Contents

Introduction

I made my first film when I was 8. It involved Lego dinosaurs with Plasticine skin terrorizing a cardboard city in glorious silent 8mm. At least, I assume it was glorious, because I don't think the film was ever developed, but in my head it will always be an epic giant monster film, up there with *Godzilla* and *Pacific Rim*.

Since then, I have spent most of my life being involved with storytelling, media and teaching, and usually a combination of all three. I've known actors, artists, writers, directors, editors and sound engineers, and from each of them I've learned something about their craft. Every one of them was passionate about what they did, and that passion rubs off.

Recently, my own passion for teaching collided with my passion for media production, and I began teaching very basic media production skills to students who were just taking their first steps out into the bigger world of media. However, this new direction also brought new challenges, as the only tools all my students had to make media with were their personal computers and their mobile phones.

What to do?

So, I learned to make movies with my mobile phone.

I talked to everyone I could, I read many articles on the subject and watched countless hours of videos online. Then, I turned it all into a series of lectures I gave to help my students prepare for their film-making projects and get the best out of what they had.

To be honest, I was shocked with what I learned.

Your Smartphone is more powerful than the computers they used to produce and edit movies like *The Phantom Menace*, *The Matrix*, *Toy Story*, and *Jurassic Park* in the 1990's.

You have in your pocket more media production power than anyone has had for 99.9% of the time humanity has been alive.

This book is about learning to use that power.

The main thing that stands between you and producing media is often not technology, but knowing a few simple skills.

In this book, you're going to learn those skills.

I'm going to teach you some of them.

You're going to teach yourselves the rest by doing it.

Welcome to the world of the Prosumer – the Producer/Consumer.

Let's go!

Who is This Book For?

This book is for people who have a passion for telling stories, but not much money. It's for anyone who wants to make their first film, and is willing to make a film using whatever they can get their hands on- mobile phone, tablet camera, digital pocket camera, DSLR, and whatever else can record video. It doesn't matter how old or young you are, the rules are the same, and the basic skills that will carry you into success are also the same.

<u>The Three Rules to Successful Indie Film-making</u>

- Plan well.
- Master your craft.
- Get out there and do it!

Terminology

Throughout this book, I'll be using a lot of film industry terms, so here's a few of the more common ones to make sure we're all on the same page-

To Shoot/To Film- These are both common terms which mean recording video using a camera of some kind.

A Shoot- Going to a place or places and recording video.

A Shot- Refers to the way in which a scene or piece of video is recorded.

A Scene- the events that happen at a particular place and time in the story.

A Take- one single recording of a scene, a shot, or a piece of a scene. (If you filmed a shot twice, it took "two takes" to film it.)

Video Clip- also known as a video file, footage, or a recording.

Standing Marks- something which shows actors where to stand during a scene, usually tape on the floor.

Diffused Light- light which is passing through something or bouncing off something before it hits the subject the camera is looking at. This kind of light often gives a better image for the camera.

Smartphone- a mobile phone which also doubles as a mini-tablet computer like the iPhone or Samsung Galaxy phones.

Feature Phone- the older style of mobile phone which are generally just a phone with a few extra features like a camera and the ability to send text messages. Most Nokia and Motorola phones fall into this category.

Chapter One: First Steps

Equipment

Someone once said, "the best camera is the one that's with you".

What does everyone have with them?

Mobile Phones.

So that's what this book is going to concentrate on. They're the thing almost everyone has, and whether it's a Feature Phone or a Smartphone, they pretty much all can take video. Now, will the video from a Nokia Feature Phone be the same as an Apple or Samsung Smartphone? Of course not. But, with a little work and understanding of how to get the best out your camera, even a Feature Phone user can produce usable video for your own personal projects.

That said, while this book focuses on using Mobile Phones for filming, the majority of it will also apply equally to Digital Pocket Cameras, DSLR Cameras, Camcorders, Handicams, Webcams, iPod Touches, MP3 Players, Tablet Cameras, and pretty much anything you can get your hands on that can shoot video.

The other reason I'm going to focus on Mobile Phones is because they're so convenient!

Think about it:

- Everyone you know likely has one, so you have multiple cameras and can film from multiple angles at the same time.
- They can fit into small and tight spaces, and film in places where a larger camera couldn't. (Like inside a mailbox or microwave, from a dashboard of a car, or corners of a room or closet.) So you can get some really interesting angles with them.
- They're Everywhere! People are so used to other people taking pictures on their phones they don't even notice them. This lets you film

without people realizing you're even doing it. This is great for filming in malls, bars and other semi-public locations without the disruption that a video camera would cause.

But, you ask, aren't mobile phone camera videos bad quality?

I mean, we've all seen that awful stuff people stick up on YouTube, and those grainy videos of something that might be Bigfoot (or your uncle- who can tell?) shambling through the woods that they show on the news from time to time.

Not at all, in fact the newest phones have really impressive cameras on them.

Don't believe me?

Watch the following short films made on 2011's iPhone 4s, and then you tell me how bad they are.

Framed by Mael Sevestre - https://vimeo.com/31013938

Operation by Film Riot- https://www.youtube.com/watch?v=I-KrhgwtXLg

Coffee Branch by Stephen de Villiers- https://vimeo.com/50726215

You can find lots more like them on YouTube as well, and this was shot on a 2011 phone! The current Smartphones from Apple and Samsung have far superior image quality to that- equal to many HD Video Cameras.

But, there is a catch. If you're going to shoot video like the people who did those films and and get those kinds of results, you're going to need to know what your phone can and can't do. You'll also need Hardware and Software, so let's get you set up!

Hardware

On the most basic level, we need you and your Mobile Phone.

But...

If you can at all manage it, it's not a bad idea to have a Tripod (you can get them for as cheap as $10 online and at some stores like Tiger Direct or Walmart). You see, tripods are super-useful, and can really improve the quality of your video just by stabilizing your camera. The sad truth is that mobile phones are super-shaky when we're holding them, and a tripod fixes that while also letting you do a lot of nifty tricks. (I'll talk specifically about Tripod Tricks in the Filming section.)

Be warned, though, while even the most cheap tripod will probably help you, tripods are a case where the more expensive the tripod is, the better video footage you will often get. This is because higher quality tripods let you turn the camera around more smoothly, whereas cheaper ones will often stick and be a little jerky when you move the camera. You can play with cheaper ones to try to work the rough spots out, but there are limits, just so you know.

Another thing you will probably need is a Mobile Phone Tripod Mount.

Most cameras have a screw hole on the bottom for mounting on tripods, but Mobile Phones don't (for obvious reasons), so we need a way to firmly and securely hold the phone on the tripod. There are a number of companies making these, and they'll be called something like a "Mobile Phone Holder" (or Bracket/Clip/Stand/Mount)- a quick search on eBay will give you over a thousand results. (Also check your local camera and electronics stores.)

Usually they sell them as part of a mini-tripod (for $20-$30) but the Mount itself can be screwed off whatever it comes with and put on pretty much any tripod using the universal screw. You can also buy the mount by itself online for as little as $3 on eBay, but the mini-tripod is pretty handy to have. The mounts themselves are semi-universal, and will fit most mobile phones, but do make sure you check the measurements of your phone and the clip before you buy them, as they might not hold some of the wider phones.

If you're a serious zero-budget filmmaker, don't have a credit card, and can't get to a store, there are a few alternatives. I've seen Do-It-Yourself Mobile Phone Mounts online that people have made from all kinds of odds and ends, including Bulldog Clips and even carved wood! Do a search on YouTube for "DIY Mobile Phone Tripod Mount" and you'll find options to suit whatever your budget is.

Extra Gear

Of course, a camera and tripod are just the start, there's a lot of other gear you might find useful.

Attachable Lenses

Many companies have produced lenses that attach to your mobile phone's own lens to give it different fields of view. You can find everything from telescopic lenses to fish-eye lenses and super-zoom lenses that will let your phone film in different ways. These attach on using special mounts, glue, or magnetic clips, and can be very useful if you want to have a wide range of shots. Many camera stores carry them, and you can find many different ones for sale on eBay, but be warned that this is another case where you will likely get what you pay for, and they can get pretty expensive at the higher end. They're really an extra, and aren't necessary, just nice to have if you can afford them.

Extra Batteries

If your phone allows the battery to be replaced, it's not a bad idea to have at least one extra battery around. Filming can often take hours, and can burn through your mobile phone's power pretty quickly. The last thing you want is to run out of power while filming a shoot and have to wait hours while the phone recharges! Extra batteries solve this problem.

Extra Memory Cards

The same as Extra Batteries. You should be buying the biggest memory card you can afford for filming, and even then have another as a backup. Filming in HD video (which you want to do if you can) goes through memory really fast, and you don't want to be caught out in the middle of a shoot with no memory space left and no place to buy more!

Things to know:

- 720p/30fps at 14 Mbps = 64mb/minute = 16 minutes video/1 GB
- 1080p/30fps at 32Mbps= 200mb/minute = 5 minutes video/1 GB
- Memory Cards are rated in "Class" from 1-10, with 1 being slowest and 10 being fastest. For shooting video, try to get the fastest possible because if your card is too slow you will have problems when recording because it can't keep up with the data being sent to it. This can even cause your recording system to crash or just stop working during a shoot.
- If you see "Ultra" it means it's rated beyond the 1-10.
- If you can, record to on-board memory and use the card for storage.

Laptops/Tablets

Laptops (or Tablets with the appropriate cords and connections) are incredibly useful when shooting with any digital device, but especially mobile phones. They allow you to offload your video from your mobile phone onto a much larger hard-drive, freeing up space, and they are mobile recharging centers for your phone as well! If you're using an iPhone, then a Laptop is even more important, as iPhones can't have extra memory cards or batteries, so the Laptop is the only way to get that video quickly off the phone so you can shoot more!

Laptops are also nice to have because they let you check the video you shoot on a larger screen, where you might spot issues that won't be easy to see on a smaller one. You can also use both Laptops and Tablets to store scripts, breakdowns, storyboards, and other shooting notes and information that you might need.

Binder

If you're oldschool (or broke) and don't have a Laptop, it's handy to keep your production documents in a binder to keep everything straight, organized and accessible. You don't want your production notes flying everywhere, do you? Or getting wet when the fake blood bags explode over everything! I also advise having a pad of Post-It Notes and some blank paper inside the Binder as well, for making notes as you're filming.

Backpacks/Camera Bags

If you have a lot of gear, you need some place to carry it safely and conveniently. A backpack is perfect for this, especially one with lots of pockets to help you be organized. Camera bags are also important if you have a higher-end camera like a DSLR or a Camcorder, because they often have attachments, and you want to make sure their lenses are safe from scratches.

Tape

On a film set, there are few things more handy and versatile than tape. Specifically, Gaffer's Tape, which comes in many colors and is made so that it attaches firmly, but then comes off without leaving a sticky residue behind that damages floors, equipment and objects. (It's this residue problem that separates Gaffer's Tape and Duct Tape. Regular Duct Tape leaves lots of residue and shouldn't be used on anything you don't want damaged by the tape. Although they do make No-Residue Duct Tape, which might be an option if you have a Home Depot or Lowes handy.) If you're just looking for something cheap for Standing Marks, you might also consider Painter's Tape. Like Gaffer's Tape it's low residue (it's made so it doesn't damage the walls and fixtures), but it's not as strong as Gaffer's Tape, so I would be careful using it to hold or attach things.

You can find Gaffer's Tape online, or ask around at your local camera or theatrical supply stores.

Lights

When filming, there is nothing more important than light. (Some will argue it's even more important than the camera you use!) I'll talk more about this later, but light is a crucial element to getting good shots, and so you need to make sure you've got good lights to work with. If you're working outdoors, you can use the sun, but if you're working indoors, proper lighting equipment is something you can't do without!

At the higher end, there are light stands and softboxes and all sorts of lighting equipment you can work with, but they also cost a lot of money. However, as a low-budget filmmaker, you can still get good basic lighting without spending a lot, in fact, you probably have what you need just around your house!

Clamp Lights and Floor Lamps are common, cheap and portable- so why not use them? Clamp lights allow for great directional light, and Floor Lamps not only provide light at different heights, but with covers on it's also a diffused light that's perfect for many lighting situations. The only issue is that the normal Incandescent Bulbs we use with them aren't usually strong enough, and sticking a high-wattage bulb past 100 watts in a normal lamp is probably not a great idea because of heat.

But there is a solution!

Compact Fluorescent Lamp (CFL) Bulbs (the twisty bulbs), that are becoming the new standard, use much lower amounts of power, produce little heat, and give off a brighter more full-spectrum light that's perfect for filming. (Some more than others, do your research.) A 30+ Watt CFL bulb can give off light equal to 150 Watt Incandescent bulb with far less power and heat, and fits easily into your floor lamps or clamp lights. The other advantage of these is that they last a long time, and can be used as general lights once filming is done.

Another alternative is to buy Work Lights from a hardware store like Home Depot or Lowes, which can be very inexpensive but incredibly bright and easy to work with. I've seen 250 Watt Worklights at Lowes for as low as $10 each, and 500 Watt lights for around $20, which makes them even cheaper than buying CFL bulbs in some cases. The only downsides are that they're very hot (use with caution!) and will often have to be diffused or bounced off something else because they're too bright.

(More on lights in the Filming section.)

Sound Recorders/Microphones

I'm not going to go into much detail about Sound Equipment because, like Cameras, that's a subject that is as deep as the ocean and can fill many books. Also, most no-budget filmmakers won't be able to afford anything but the most basic and cheapest options anyways, so there isn't much point. However, there are a few things that are good for beginners to know.

Generally speaking, you don't want to use the microphones built into your camera or mobile phone for recording your audio unless you have to.

Built-in microphones can't hear actors unless they're right in front of you, but somehow still manage to pick up every noise in the environment that you don't want them to hear. If you want quality audio, you want to either plug a microphone into the camera's input, or you want a separate sound recording device.

The main thing to know about Microphones is that there are two main types- Dynamic and Condenser.

Dynamic Microphones are the ones people scream into at Karaoke night and while they are cheaper, they're also much shorter ranged and pick up a lower range of sound as well. In film production, Dynamic microphones are usually used is as Lavalier Mics (aka Lavaliers, Lavs, Lapel Mics, Clip Mics or Personal Mics) which are hidden on the actor's body around the collar and feed into a sound recorder also hidden on or near the actor.

Condenser Microphones are the more powerful full-range microphones- they're bigger and pick up pretty much everything in the direction they're pointed at in strong, clear detail. In film production, these are what are used for external microphones on cameras and as part of Boom Microphones which are held just off camera to pick up what the actors are saying. As you might suspect, these are much more expensive than Dynamic Microphones, and at a minimum will likely cost you around $100 and up for a new one. (And price = quality.)

The other option you should know about is Sound Recording Devices, which also have two kinds that interest us.

Digital Voice Recorders are small, relatively cheap (under $100) devices with built-in microphones that are meant for recording things like personal notes and college lectures. They can be hidden on the actors and paired with lavalier microphones to record what each actor is saying to mix together later in editing. Their sound quality often isn't as good as a full digital audio recorder, but they're cheap and easy to find, which is the important part.

Handheld Digital Audio Recorders, like those made by ZOOM, BOSS, Edriol and M-Audio are the big brothers to the Digital Voice Recorders. They have much higher quality condenser microphones on them that catch and record professional level stereo sound, and have many more options to control what sound is recorded and how it's captured. They can be used on the actors, on boom poles, or pretty much anyplace you want to hide them to record sound. As you might suspect, they start at around $200 and go up from there, but if you have the money, one of these is worth its weight in gold for your production's audio quality. Go find samples and comparisons online and judge for yourself.

Dollies

A Dolly is a wheeled platform where the camera (and possibly its operator) sits so that they can be moved around smoothly while recording. Sometimes the camera will sit on a tripod on the dolly and the camera operator will push it along, and other times the operator and the camera will both be on the dolly and another person will move then. Professional dollies also often have tracks which are laid out before filming to make sure that the camera follows a particular pattern of movement for a particular shot.

While Dollies might seem like something that are way outside the realm of no-budget film-making, this isn't true at all. In fact, anything with wheels the camera, tripod, or its operator can be placed on while filming can act as a dolly and allow you to take moving shots, the only limit is your creativity. This can really up your production value, and allows smooth pan-in shots with mobile phone cameras that can't zoom well while filming.

A few examples of DIY Dollies are:

- Tripods with non-stick pads or cloth underneath the feet (for indoor shooting over short distances)

- Skateboards (for low-down action shots)
- Wheelchairs (lock the front wheels forward if possible)
- Wheelbarrows (great for off-road shots)
- Shopping Carts (stealing is bad, don't do it!)
- Office Chairs (noisy, but good for video-only shots)
- Bicycles (have someone hold you while you ride slowly and film, a Bollywood favorite!)
- Motorcycles (noisy, but do-able)
- Electric Bikes (quieter than motorcycles)
- Cars (don't drive and dolly at the same time!)

Stabilizer Rigs

The last item that no-budget filmmakers might want to look into are stabilizer rigs- these are frames and devices which are designed to minimize the amount of shaking and unwanted movement while filming handheld. This can be really important if you want to be able to follow moving targets while producing usable video, especially with mobile phones. There are many different kinds of stabilizers, and the professionally built ones run $100 and up.

For the no-budget filmmaker who is a little bit handy or creative, however, there are many different tutorial videos on YouTube which can tell you how to make a wide variety of Camera Stabilizers for the cost of US$3 to US$30 and a little bit of time. Give them a look, they might improve your video quality a lot if you have many running/action scenes.

Software

Having the right software can make a big difference in the quality of your final video, but just as important is finding something that works for you, and knowing how to use it. Make sure you test out several different kinds of software and APPs for your mobile phone and editing platform to find the right ones for you, and then practice with them as much as possible so you understand them inside and out before using them to film your projects.

Mobile Phone APPs

If you're using an iPhone or Android Smartphone, then you need to know that the basic camera video recording app isn't your best option for video. The camera apps were designed first and foremost to take still photographic shots, and video was something they didn't expect people to take much of. As a result, the basic video recording applications don't give you the kind of control you need for recording high quality material, and you should invest in something better if you want to get the most out of your phone's camera.

I should point out now that for whatever reason, APP developers seem to think that iPhone users love their cameras and want to record and edit on them all the time, whereas they think Android users have almost no interest in the subject. As a result, the options for Android OS users are pretty limited.

Video Recording

For iPhone users, there are several APPs out there on the iTunes Store, but there is one APP that is currently so far above the others that it has become the standard alternative to the built-in camera APP- *Filmic Pro*. If you want to record high quality video on an iPhone you need to get this APP and learn to use it, it's that simple. I'll talk more about *Filmic Pro* later in the Production section.

However, if you don't like *Filmic Pro* for whatever reason, there are a few other alternatives worth looking at. *Vizzywig* is a very full-featured video recording AND editing app, and is very impressive, if a little expensive. (Get it while it's on sale.) Or, there's *MoviePro*, which is the cheapest of the three, but is a little more limited in terms of on-screen control over your camera.

For Android users, the choice is much less clear. There are a number of APPs in the Marketplace which can give you better recording options than the basic camera APP, but none that stand out like *Filmic Pro* does for the iPhone. One program I've seen recommended for filming video is *IG Camera Pro*, but you'll have to try it and others for yourself to see which one works best for you.

Audio Recording

iPhone users have a few options for stand-alone audio recording programs, but the one I recommend trying is the *RODE REC LE* audio recording APP. It's free, but despite being free it does a great job of recording and saves the audio files in a variety of formats, include lossless ones like AIFF.

Android users again have many to choose from, and so far I've been unable to find any that stand out above the others when it comes to stand-alone audio recorders. Your best bet is to read reviews and try a few out to find one that works for you.

Video Editing

On the iPhone the video editor of choice is unsurprisingly *iMovie*, although the phone version isn't as full-featured as the desktop one. *Splice* is a good alternative, and a bit cheaper. There is also *Cinefy*, which is actually made to add pre-built special effects to your videos if you want to liven them up by having yourself chased by a T-Rex, it has over 100 of them built-in. (In fact, there are a lot of special iPhone apps just for adding FX, changing colors, or otherwise modifying your video once you shoot it. Explore and have fun with them!)

On Android phones, it's really hard to give any recommendations. There are some APPs that do allow editing on your phone, but none stand out. You can search around the marketplace for programs with good reviews, but you're likely better off editing on your computer instead.

Scriptwriting

In theory, you can use any program to write a script that lets you put words onto a screen- *MS WORD, PAGES, Open Office, Google Docs*, even *Wordpad*- anything can be used to write a script. Also, if you're just writing a script for yourself to use in your own production, it pretty much doesn't matter what your script looks like so long as you and everyone else involved can understand it.

So, why use scriptwriting software, then?

Well, for most scripts, the people who write them aren't the same people as the ones who actually use them in the end to make a movie. So, to make things simple, Hollywood developed a bunch of format and style rules so that everyone knew the "right" way to produce a script. This is what's known as "the industry standard", and if your goal is to someday share scripts outside of your circle of friends (and maybe sell them), then you might as well learn it now. Using it also makes you look more like a professional in the eyes of others, like people you want helping you make this film, and shows you're serious about your projects.

In Hollywood, the standard go-to Scriptwriting software of choice is *Final Draft*, with *Movie Magic Screenwriter* coming up a close second. Both of these very powerful programs will take care of all the formatting for you, and have all sorts of extras that will help you plan, edit and revise your scripts until they shine.

Unfortunately, they also cost a lot of money.

But, luckily for you, there are two free alternatives now available: *CELTX* and *Trebly*

CELTX (pronounced Kell-Tex) works on PC, MAC or LINUX, and is an all-purpose writer-director-producer toolkit for movie makers. At its most basic level, it's a scriptwriting program, but it also helps you organize your production, make storyboards, break down your script into the things you need to make it into a film, and even lets you set up schedules, print off call sheets, and tag locations. How much or little of this power you want to use is up to you, but the basics will take you minutes to learn, and there are hundreds of tutorials online to tell you how to do almost anything you can ask *CELTX* to help you with. (There is a paid version with extra enhancements like online workspaces that you can share with friends and co-writers, but it's not required to use the software.)

Get it at Celtx.com

Trebly is for PC and LINUX, and is a much simpler program than *CELTX*- being a pure scriptwriting program. There's not a lot I can say about *Trebly* except that it works, exports to any format you could want, and is easy to use. If all you want is something to quickly write scripts on, this might be the program for you!

Get it at Trebly.org

Video Editing

Once you've got your filming done, you'll need something to put it together with. For this, you'll need a video editing program on your computer. There are free, mid-range and high-end options for both MAC and PC.

Free

Windows Movie Maker (PC) - WMM has been around for a long time and has evolved over the years from a glitchy and annoying piece of software into something very simple and user friendly. It allows you to edit clips, string clips together, insert transitions, add music and narration, and export the files into your format of choice, all while still being very easy to use. It's not a bad program, and if your needs are simple, it may be exactly what you need, so try it out!

iMovie (MAC) - Similar to Windows Movie Maker for Macs, a good simple program for easily clipping, editing, and putting together basic videos without a lot of FX. Probably one of the most user-friendly video editors ever made.

Lightwave (PC/MAC) - is a piece of high-end, paid video editing software that has since gone free. It's extremely powerful, has even been used to edit Hollywood movies, and can do a great many things a simple program like Windows Movie Maker can't. However, it was designed for professionals by professionals, and even though it's free it wasn't designed with user-friendliness in mind. The maker has also released a series of very good tutorial videos, and if you want to use Lightwave well you'll need them.

Cinelerra (LINUX) - A high-powered fully-functional video editing program similar to Lightwave, but only for Linux machines.

Kdenlive (MAC/LINUX) - Another fairly basic free video editing program, however this one allows for multi-track editing and has more advanced features than iMovie or WMM. *Kdenlive* is open-source and supported by a community instead of a big company.

Jahshaka (PC/MAC/LINUX) - Another multi-track editor like *Kdenlive*, and also both open source and community driven.

Blender (PC/LINUX/MAC) - *Blender* is actually a 3-D graphics program, but it has a good multi-track editing suite built into it that can be used like any of the others on this list. This is another one with a steep learning curve, but *Blender* can do so much more than video editing that some people might consider the time worth it. (If you're geeky and ambitious, go for it!)

Mid-Range (Paid under $100)

Mid-Range Video Editing Software balances power and user-friendliness, and is aimed at the hobbyist and home-user, rather than professionals. That doesn't mean it can't produce high quality work just like a professional grade program does, it just means they don't have as many extras as the high grade programs do for playing with your video clips. If you have the money, and need something better than *iMovie* or *Windows Movie Maker*, these would be the ones worth investing in.

Adobe Premiere Elements (PC/MAC) - A stripped-down version of the industry standard PC video editing program *Adobe Premiere Pro*. Multi-track editing, special effects, text effects, and compatible with everything you're likely to try to edit with it. If you're willing to pay, need something simple to use, and don't need a high-end video editing program this isn't a bad choice.

SONY Movie Studio (PC) - Similar to *Premiere Elements*, this is the simplified version of the *SONY VEGAS* professional-grade video editing suite. A little less user friendly than the other two mid-range programs, but has a lot of features, and comes with a huge collection of Special FX built into it.

Cyberlink Powerdirector (PC) - Not as well known as *Premiere Elements* or *Sony Movie Studio*, Powerdirector is probably the most versatile and powerful of the Mid-Range video editing programs, and is as close to a professional level program you can get for under $100. One neat feature is that it comes with a full suite of royalty free music, and will generate soundtracks on its own for you to accompany your video. It's extremely easy to use, and has a large number of tutorials online you can access for help if you need it.

Professional Grade ($300+)

At the professional level, there are really just three programs worth mentioning: *Sony VEGAS Pro* (PC), *Adobe Premiere Pro* (PC/MAC) and *Final Cut Pro* (MAC) Each of them has been around for years and earned their reputations as part of the entertainment industry. Naturally, they are all outside the budget of no-budget filmmakers, but I wanted to mention them regardless. Which one you use is largely a matter of taste and style, as with any of the three the only real limits are the user, not the software. If you've been using Adobe or Sony's entry-level editors, then maybe you'll find their big brothers familiar and quick to learn, and each has free limited time trials you can play with to find out which works best for you.

Cloud Video Editors

As I write this, a new type of video editing program has recently appeared- one based in The Cloud rather than your PC, and accessed through your browser. This allows them to work on any computer which can connect to the Internet, and also allows people to collaborate on-line on video editing projects.

Of special interest is *YouTube Video Editor*, which is essentially a Cloud-based version of *Windows Movie Maker* at the moment. It's just started, however, and will probably become more advanced as time goes on, so check it out and keep an eye on it. There is another slightly more advanced up-and-comer called *WeVideo* that shows a lot of potential as well, and might be worth taking a look at.

Audio Editing

Film-making is as much about the audio as it is about the video, and quite a bit of work often ends up going into making the audio of a film sound as good as possible. Music, sound effects and narration can all be extremely important parts of the film-making process, and you need to be able to control them as well as you can control what the audience sees. While many video editors also allow you to do some work with sound, you will find you often need finer control or advanced features, and for this, you may need Audio Editing Software.

Free

The good news is that for free audio editing software, you don't have to look very far. *Audacity* is a free, open-source audio editing program that runs on PC, MAC, Linux, and pretty much everything else. It does multi-track editing, has vast numbers of plug-ins, and is overall very easy to use. It's become the go-to software for beginning audio engineers of all stripes- so make it yours, watch a tutorial or two, and you'll be off and running.

If you have a MAC, then you already likely have *Garageband*, which will also suit you pretty well. If you want an alternative to *Audacity* or *Garageband*, there are quite a few, just run a search for "Free Audio Editor" and you'll find many which might suit you.

Paid

If you're feeling like investing in audio editing software because you need something more powerful than *Audacity*, there are a few choices, although none of them come cheap. When I first started working with audio, *Audacity* was still in its infancy, so I used *Adobe Audition* (PC/MAC) which is a good choices for those who need finer control over things like Noise

Removal. There is also *Cubase* (PC/MAC) and Avid's *Pro Tools* (PC/MAC) which are professional grade software.

(Robert) Rodriguez List

When the American Director Robert Rodriguez decided to make his first full film, *El Mariachi*, the first thing he did (even before writing the script) was sit down and make a list of all the possible resources he had available to him.

He did this because he knew if he wanted to make the best film he could for the little money available, he had to make the best possible use of all the resources he could get his hands on. He felt that if he just used what he had, instead of worrying about what he didn't have, he could produce a much better film.

He was right, *El Mariachi* was made for $7000, and would later catapult him into Hollywood success as a man who could produce quality work for a budget. He chronicles this in his book *Rebel Without a Crew*, which is good reading for any aspiring filmmaker.

Later on, in the book *DV Rebel's Guide* (also more good reading), Stu Maschwitz would use the term "Robert Rodriguez List" to describe following Rodriguez's approach and making a list of all your assets and resources before you start to plan your first film.

I recommend you do the same.

Whether you know what you want to make, or are just trying to come up with something worth making, sit down and make a Rodriguez List beforehand. In it, try to include every single relevant asset you have available to you, up to and including...

- Camera Gear (Mobile Phone, DSLR Camera, Webcam, whatever can film!)
- Sound Gear
- Software

- Your skills/talents
- Your strengths and weaknesses
- Places to film you have access to in one way or another.
- Vehicles
- Clothes (especially special or unique stuff)
- Lights
- Props (Swords, Wheelchairs, Umbrellas, anything useful)
- Set Decorations
- Makeup
- People who can act.
- People who like you.
- People who owe you favors.
- People who know people who can act.
- People who have equipment you could use.
- People who have access to locations to film.
- People who can help you carry your gear or drive you around.
- People who you can consult/ask for help in your weak areas.

Basically, you're listing anything or anyone you think might be remotely useful in making a film. It doesn't matter whether you use it or not, this list helps you have a realistic idea of what you can pull off before you start to plan. Even if you don't use something from the list on this project, you might end up using it on the next one!

One tip with shooting locations- remember that what looks boring and commonplace to you might still look exotic and interesting to someone who lives far away from you. Don't always think you need locations that look exotic and different to you, because they might look boring and uninteresting to others! I used to journey to work past the World's Tallest Building everyday, so to me it was normal and uninteresting, but thousands of people from across the planet traveled to see it every day!

Chapter Two: Preparing to Film

Doing it Right

I know a lot of you are just chomping at the bit to film, and can't wait to get out there and shoot, but there's something you need to understand. The more I've studied about film-making, the more I've come to realize it's about preparation. It's about that hundred little things you do before the camera ever rolls that make the difference between something that looks amateur and something that looks professional. From the script, to casting, to storyboarding, to finding the right props, to costuming- all of these (and so much more) are what you see on screen without realizing it. It's about balancing careful preparation with filming, and the more you up the filming and lower the prep, the worse your production will be for it.

Take the time, and do it right.

The results will be worth it.

Project Style

One thing to think about when you start planning your film is what style you intend to work in. For some films, the traditional Narrative style is best, but there are other options, for example the Found Footage Genre might be a better fit for some projects.

Narrative- Almost every movie you've ever seen in the theater or on TV was a narrative film, a film which tells a fictional story through a series of scenes, edits, camera movements, etc. There are different styles and types of narrative films, but for our purposes a narrative film is one which tells a narrative (a story) in a straightforward manner.

The advantage to narrative films is that you can do almost anything with them you can envision, as long as you remember that video is a visual medium. You can be as realistic, dramatic, detailed or abstract as you want, and it's a blank canvas for you to fill with your own artistic vision.

The disadvantage of narrative film is that your audience has been watching them their wholes lives, and thus has pre-set ideas about what they are and how they should look. A no-budget film-maker can't produce Hollywood-level films in terms of production values, it just isn't going to happen, and this will turn some of your potential audience off right from the start. You're going to have to be very creative to play off your strengths and minimize your weaknesses to make a narrative film that a general audience will accept.

Found Footage- The "Found Footage" genre effectively started with the *Blair Witch Project*, and has since evolved from there. In essence, a Found Footage film is supposed to be showing a collection of film and video clips that are recordings of "real" events that someone has captured in the past. This can be anything from video diaries or journals, to security camera video, to (fake) documentary recordings, to (fake) news clips or video taken on the fly by people to show their friends. Generally, most Found Footage films are Horror movies, but there have been Science Fiction (*Europa Report*), Adventure (*Trollhunter*), Giant Monster (*Cloverfield*), Dramas (*Look*) and even Superhero (*Chronicle*) Found Footage films as well.

The advantage to Found Footage films for no-budget filmmakers is that the audience doesn't expect Hollywood-level production values from them. This is supposed to be video taken with everyday cameras of varying quality in different lighting conditions with questionable sound, so the audience accepts this as adding realism to what they're watching. The same goes for the acting- these are supposed to be real people, not actors. (Although outright bad acting will still produce bad results.)

The disadvantage is that you're locked into presenting "reality", and usually in a very limited way. You can't do many fancy shots, you can't play with drama, editing or sound in a major way, and you're stuck with "realistic" recordings of the events. Found Footage also tends to work better for some genres than others, but in theory could be used for any genre with enough creativity on your part.

If you want to do a Found Footage film, go watch as many of them as you can so that you know the "rules", because audiences now have certain expectations of them. Also, while the video may suck, try to make sure you have fairly good audio, because while people will sit through bad video, they won't stand bad audio very long.

Scriptwriting

Someone once asked Director Alfred Hitchcock what three things it took to make a great film.

His answer?

"The script, the script, and the script."

While he might be underestimating the value of the many other skills involved in making a film good, he's still right about one thing- the script is the foundation of any film. It is the document which will decide if a film gets made, how difficult it is to make, and whether the final product will be any good.

In short, if your script sucks- so will your film.

Scriptwriting, like any craft, takes a lifetime to master, but hopefully I can help kickstart you on the process.

Screenplay Structure

As a general rule, screenplays can be broken down into five parts.

- Lines/Actions (the words and actions of the actors and things on screen)
- Shots (the specific images we see on the screen, close-up, wide shot, etc)
- Scenes (collections of lines and shots telling an event)
- Sequences (collections of scenes telling a story)
- Acts (sections of the overall story- beginning, middle and end)

Of these five parts, when you first start writing you should only worry about three of them- Lines/Actions, Scenes and Acts. Shots are something you can worry about when you do storyboarding, shot lists, or breakdowns (unless you have a good idea of what the shot will be when writing the script, in which case go ahead and note it!) and Sequences are something you'll master later as you get more practice at writing scripts.

So, let's talk more about the other three.

Lines/Actions

These are the words spoken by the actors (dialog) and the things that happen to them and the other objects we see on the screen (actions).

Dialog: Bob: "I wish I'd worn my sunglasses. Gonna be a scorcher."

Action: Bob steps out into the sunlight and raises his hand to shade his eyes.

These are the heart of the story, the basic building blocks we use to compose each scene, and eventually make the whole film itself. If you can describe people saying and doing things, then congrats! You can write a film. It really is that easy.

A few Tips about writing Lines/Actions

- Write as little dialog as you can possibly get away with, try to tell the story in images and visual actions as much as possible.
- Every line should 1) Establish Character and 2) Move the Plot Forward.
- Don't be overly specific with your action descriptions- keep them as simple as possible as well. Don't write "It's an old basement room in a residential house that looks like it hasn't been decorated in twenty years, with old peeling wallpaper, chipped paint and flatted down plush carpet." (unless those details are important to the story) Instead, write "it's a room" or "it's an old room". You're not writing a novel, and details like that can be sorted out in pre-production later on. The more detail you write, the harder (and more expensive) it becomes to make that detail into reality.
- Don't be too specific when describing characters either. "Barbara, a middle aged blonde woman, is walking up the front steps," is fine, you don't need to tell us her life story, and it also makes casting easier.
- Always write all actions in present tense. "He is eating bread" not "He was eating bread," for example. Write it like it's happening on the screen right now! It's not a past event, it's live and immediate. It will make your script more interesting to read.

Scenes

In essence, a scene is a telling of events which happen at a particular place and time. It usually has a beginning, a middle, and an end, and tells the audience some or all of the things that happened during that period of time. Examples of scenes might be two friends walking along and discussing a third friend, a pot of water boiling, or a man playing with his dog. Once the time period changes, or the location changes, the scene is finished as well.

Scenes are the building blocks of the story as a whole, and it's by stringing scenes together that we make films. For example, we have a scene where two characters meet, then another scene of their first date, and finally a scene of them getting married. Individually these scenes may just be events, but they can become parts of a greater story by working together.

The reason for scenes is twofold:

1. To keep the story concise and moving. (We don't have time to watch everything, so scenes serve as little windows in time to the events unfolding.)
2. In production, each change of location can have various requirements (ie lights and cameras for film) and breaking things down into scenes makes production easier. (Something you may not realize is that most movies are not shot in script order, but based on what scenes are best shot at a particular location and time.)

Tips for writing Scenes

- Generally speaking, try to keep each scene in a story under three pages of script format. Three pages of script is roughly three minutes of screentime, and while it doesn't seem like much, it's a lot of time to spend on a single scene. You want to keep your story interesting and moving, and letting your scenes go on too long is a sure way to slow things down. (Again, this is a general rule, not the word of god.)
- Every scene should 1) Establish Character and 2) Move the Plot Forward.

Acts

The idea of Acts comes from Greek Dramas, which broke plays up into Acts as a way to allow for costume and scene changes. In the old days of theatre, each Act was a major change in time and location, and then the next series of Scenes would occur at that new location.

Today, we use the term Acts as a structural term to describe the different phases of a story. Used this way, each Act can be said to represent a major change in the direction of the plot.

The most common structure in all of storytelling is the 3-Act structure-

- Beginning
- Middle
- End

We use this structure because we're human, and those are the phases of a human being's life. The 3 Act Structure was first discussed by Aristotle in his book called *Poetics* in 335 BCE, which described an "incline" and structure that a drama must have to be interesting.

So you see, none of this is exactly new!

Act 1 is the Introduction.

It sets up the story for everything else to follow. It introduces the characters, situations, and any anything else the audience needs to know to understand the story. This is where you hook your audience, making them interested in the story and characters.

Generally speaking, a script starts by introducing the situation and the main character, and then introduces a challenge that this main character must overcome. The character and the challenge they need to overcome will be the backbone of the story, and when they overcome that challenge the story is over. Once that character has decided to face their challenge in some way and is locked on course, we enter Act Two.

Act Two is about The Struggle.

Our characters and situations have been introduced, now the real conflict of the story begins. The longest of the three acts, this is where our main character begins their uphill struggle to try to overcome their challenge. They do this by making choices, and while some of these choices will go very well, most of them will probably go pretty poorly, or have unexpected negative consequences.

Around the end of Act Two, everything that can go wrong, does go wrong. Characters die (or are put into critical condition), loved ones are lost, hope turns to despair, etc.

The main character is usually left an emotional wreck who must now deal with the new harsh reality. This is where we enter Act Three.

Act Three is about Resolution.

In this Act the main character deals with the events of the end of Act Two, and chooses the direction that will ultimately take them headlong into the climax of the story. In the climax, the main character faces their greatest challenge and (presumably) defeats it in an epic physical, emotional or psychological battle.

This can be as physical as beating up the bad guy, or as emotional as accepting that you need someone else in your life. Whatever the events, they have be the results of a decision made by the main character, or as a consequence of the decisions they have made throughout the story.

In the end, by overcoming that final challenge the main character's life now enters a new phase, and the main character often becomes a new person, changed by the events of the story in some significant way.

How much time should your script spend on each of these? Well, the very rough general rule is 25%/50%/25%. So, if your script is 20 minutes (20 pages in script format) long, then your introduction (Act 1) should be around 5 pages, your middle (Act 2) should be around 10 pages, and your end (Act 3) should be around 5 pages. If they go over or under, it's okay, these are just rough guides.

What's a Story?

As a writing teacher, one of the biggest hurdles I've found my students often have to face when writing scripts has been that they don't know what a story is. When I say this, you might laugh, but think about it right now- what is a story? How would you define one?

Not so easy, is it?

Alright, let's use an example-

John walks into a room, shoots Sam, and leaves.

Is this a story?

Why or why not?

It has a beginning, middle and end.

It has two people.

One of them is doing something.

So, does that make it a story?

No, it's not a story (at least by my definition), it's a Vignette. A Vignette is a brief moment in time, like a painting or a few seconds of film. There is no conflict, no characters, no motivations, no choices. It could work as part of a larger story, but it isn't a story by itself.

Okay then, how about this one?

John walks into a room, talks about how Sam betrayed him, shoots him, and leaves.

How about this? Is this a story?

Nope, this is an Event.

We have character and motivation now, but we still lack a crucial ingredient- conflict. John has explained his reasons, but there is no conflict between the characters or within them. This is still a telling of an Event, not a Story. This is like a scene from a history book, or a documentary where we're watching footage of real events which were captured on film. Things are happening, there might be characters, but nobody is making any serious choices, and there's no real conflict.

Okay, another one...

John walks into a room, puts his gun in front of him on the table and tells Sam he has sixty seconds to explain why John shouldn't shoot him for killing his brother. Sam fails. John shoots him and leaves.

Yes, as you probably guessed, <u>this is a story</u>.
We have a beginning, middle, and end.
We have character and motivation.
We have conflict!
John is trying to make a choice within himself about whether to shoot Sam.
Sam is trying to find a way to live.
The audience is interested, and has a clear question in their minds- "Will John shoot him?"

So, you can see what makes a story is characters making choices- the harder, the better! If a character isn't making choices, hard choices with consequences, then it's not a story, it's a vignette or a series of events. (Or, at best, it's a really boring story!)

But, there's one more element, in addition to Choices, there must be a consequence to whether the character wins or loses- some Stakes. And, they must be something that will affect the character, and hopefully also affect the audience as well. (Through our attachment to the character, if possible.) Without stakes there's no tension and no reason to worry about the character or what's happening. (In other words- no reason to pay attention to the story.)

The smaller the stakes, the more important it is that the audience is attached to the character.

The larger the stakes, the less important, but it still makes a big difference if the audience cares about the characters involved.

You will also note that both of the previous things, Choices and Stakes, come from within Characters. Characters are the core of a story, not events, and the characters in a story must choose the events that lead to the end of the story. In a story, a good story, thing happen because of the characters and the choices they have made. Think back to your favorite movies, and think about the choices the characters made- did they affect the story? How?

I think you'll find that their decisions had a huge effect on the shape of the story and how the story ended, which is exactly why you enjoyed the movie so much.

So, why not write your story that way too?

In closing...

A Vignette

- Pronounced "Vin-Yet"
- A snapshot or brief moment in time captured in the form of media (photo, text, film, etc).
- A scene in a story can be a vignette if taken out of the story and its greater context.
- A Vignette may or may not have a beginning, middle or end.
- It usually doesn't have a conflict of any significance to the characters involved. (Definitely no Stakes involved.)
- It may or may not have a sense of character.
- Examples- A girl sitting smoking on a park bench. A dog and his master playing. A man making breakfast and serving it.

An Event

- An Event is the telling of a series of things happening, usually in order.
- Again, it can be part of a larger story (usually as a Sequence), but becomes an event when removed from the larger context.
- It will often have a beginning, middle, and end.
- It will usually have characters.
- It may have motivations.
- It may have conflict, but these are obstacles (like speedbumps) rather than conflicts requiring actual emotions and serious decision

making.

- Examples- A runner running a race. A drunk trying to find his keys and get into his house. A man walking to get his mail. Two men robbing a bank without any problems between them or in their robbery plan.
- The truth is, watching events is actually a bit boring because we don't have any emotional investment in them, so unless there's something to keep us interested, our minds wander. It's also why opening a story with a 20 page battle scene before we're introduced to the characters is generally a bad idea. (And why very few people have actually managed to read *The Silmarillion* all the way through!)
- Cool visuals or art in a short film can make watching an event interesting. (Although usually not for long films.)
- Interactivity (video games) which brings you into an event and makes you part of it can also keep it interesting. (Most video games are actually Interactive Events, not Character-Driven Stories. If you transcribed most Video Games into a story, the results would usually be pretty dull and uninteresting. They're only cool while you're a part of the game because you're providing the emotional core.)

A Story

- A story is the telling of a series of events which surround a character trying to achieve a goal which is not easy for them to achieve.
- It requires a beginning, middle and end. (Or at least resolution.)
- It requires characters with stated or implied motivations.
- It often involves change on the part of a main character. Emotional change (gaining love, recovering from loss), social change (money, status) or physical change (prison, death).
- Some would argue that a story without a significant element of change isn't a story at all.
- Examples- Two friends fighting over the same girl. A boy trying to rescue his pet from bullies. A girl trying to cheer up her best friend after a bad breakup. A man trying to lead a group of survivors through a zombie-filled landscape. A dwarf trying to become a king during a medieval kingdom's civil war.

In Summary...

- Two men in a truck waiting to rob a bank. (Vignette.)
- Two men robbing a bank with little to no difficulty. (Event)
- An innocent pacifist being blackmailed to rob a bank by his ex-friend who also orders him to kill the security guard during the robbery. (Story)

- Character+Goals+Stakes+Choices = Story

Building an Action-Based Story

Avoiding the dreaded "Series of Events" problem.

Michael walked into a room, and then shot Bob, and then walked out.

This is an "event", it's stuff happening without any dramatic element to keep the audience interested in what's going on. In short bursts this can be fine (like a single scene), but if you want to keep your audience engaged it can be murder to your story.

Three words.

Trey Parker and Matt Stone (creators of *South Park*, and *Team America*) offer a simple solution to this problem- view a story as a series of cause and effect events, and reflect that in your plotting.

Replace "and then" with one of these three:

- But
- And So (or Therefore)
- Meanwhile

See the Difference?

Old- Michael walked into a room, and then shot Bob, and then walked out.

New- Michael walked into a room to shoot Bob, but Bob was waiting for him, and so the two had a firefight and Bob was shot, but now the police were on their way, and so Michael needed to escape, but the police arrived before Michael could reach his car, therefore Michael had to find a place to hide and ran into Rachel's office, but...

We could go on from here as long as needed in a chain of cause and effect.

Inaction Scenes

This works within a scene, but it's also a great way to structure stories between scenes.

1. Michael finds he has no milk and then Michael leaves his house.
2. (and then) Michael goes to the store.
3. (and then) Michael buys milk.
4. (and then) Michael pays for it and chats with the clerk.
5. (and then) Michael drives home.
6. (and then) Michael eats breakfast.

These are all "and then" scenes, strung together like a series of events. And then, the audience got bored and left...

Let's try using "but" and "and so" to connect them.

1. Michael finds he's out of milk, and so he goes to the store.
2. But at the first store they're out of milk.
3. Therefore, Michael goes to another store.
4. But, on the way he sees a car accident.
5. And so he stops to help and gets involved in the rescue operation.
6. But fuel is leaking from the car, which is on fire, and so he needs to get the passengers out quickly, but they're trapped...

Using "But" and "And So" almost forces you as a writer to build conflict into the story.

Another Example- Jack and the Beanstalk

1. Jack and his mother need food,
2. And so, he is sent to buy bread.
3. But, Jack meets a seller on the road who convinces him to buy some Magic Beans.
4. And so, when he goes home his mother is angry and throws the

beans out the window.

5. But, when the beans hit dirt, they turn into a giant beanstalk.
6. And so, Jack decides to find out where the beanstalk goes.
7. But, when he gets to the top he finds an evil giant's castle.
8. And so, Jack is forced to flee back down the stalk.
9. But, the giant is coming after him.
10. And so, he cuts down the stalk and the giant falls to his death.
11. But, everyone is happy the giant is dead
12. And so, Jack becomes a hero.

Meanwhile

Of course, most stories don't just follow one character or line of plot, they often also follow other lines.

This is where Meanwhile comes in...

1. Michael discovers he's out of milk, and so he goes to the store.
2. Meanwhile, Bob and Kyle get ready to rob a grocery store.
3. And so when Michael gets to the store, Bob and Kyle are in the middle of robbing it.
4. But Michael is an off-duty police officer, and so he takes out his gun and tries to stop the robbery.
5. But Bob spots Michael, and Michael is shot in the shoulder and so Bob leaves him to die on the deli floor.
6. Meanwhile, the police respond to the alarm, and so....

The chain of cause an effect continues, and Meanwhile allows you to have multiple chains of Cause and Effect going on at the same time.

And So...

When you're planning a story, trying writing each whole scene out as a single sentence. (Or, writing out the events of each scene as a series of sentences.) See if there are "and then" or "but/and so" connections between them. If you find many "and then" connections, it likely means you're just telling a series of events and not a story. Try to find a way to make most of them "but" or "and so" connections.

But...

If all the "buts" are because of outside events being done to the characters, the story will feel like God picking on them, not an interesting story about a person navigating through life. You should try to mix it up so that the "buts" are coming from a mix of physical, mental/emotional, and social reasons based around the character.

Physical- Michael can't eat pizza because he's allergic to tomatoes.

Mental- Michael can't eat pizza because he's on a diet.

Social- Michael can't eat pizza because he forgot to bring his wallet, and he's too embarrassed to tell his friends he can't pay for it.

Meanwhile...

Be aware that it is still possible to write a really boring story using this method. You still need a character making choices at the center of it, not just events. Things happening to a well defined character and watching them deal with it are what makes stories interesting. Also remember that "and so" includes characters changing as a result of "buts", and those are often the most interesting stories of all!

Dialog

For many people, one of the hardest parts of scriptwriting is dialog- two people just talking to each other. They worry that their characters sound fake, or awkward, or worse- all sound the same! This is a completely natural fear, likely because it's true.

Good dialog is really hard to write, and that's why Hollywood writers get paid the big bucks. But, hard doesn't mean impossible, and it doesn't mean you can't do it too!

You just need to understand a few fundamental concepts, the first of which is that dialog is not real language! Like Reality TV and Pro-Wrestling, it's a created thing disguised as something real, and hiding its true fake roots underneath! And, once you learn to spot dialog and the difference, you'll be on your way to writing it.

So, let's look at some examples.

Is this dialog?

Al: Are you going to the store?
Bob: Yes. Do you want something?
Al: Can you buy a bottle of coke?
Bob: Sure. No problem.

Or, how about this?

Al: Hey man, off to the store?

Bob: (cheerful) You know it! Jenny's coming over tonight and I need to get some fixin's so I can make dinner for her.

Al: Well, I guess we know who's going to be worshiping the Porcelain God tonight! Can you grab a 2 litre of Coke for me?

Bob: You promise to be out of here by six?

Al: Scouts honor. I can't stand the sound of barfing.
Bob: I hate you.
Al: But Snuggles! I thought we had something special?
Bob: (sighs) Just be gone by six.

As I'm sure you suspect, the answer is #2 is dialog, while #1 isn't. The reason? Well, let's look at what Dialog does.

Good dialog reveals:

- Character
- Motivation
- Conflict
- Story
- Background

Generally speaking, every line spoken in a story should be doing a minimum of two of these things. That's a minimum, not a maximum. If your words are only doing one, they're slacking off and you need to whip 'em good!

So, let's look at that first exchange again...

Al: Are you going to the store?
Bob: Yes. Do you want something?
Al: Can you buy a bottle of coke?
Bob: Sure. No problem.

- Character? Well, we have some names, but there's no personality in those lines. They could be spoken by anyone, anywhere.
- Motivation? Well, Al desires a bottle of coke, so that's something.
- Conflict? Al asks for Coke and gets it. Not much conflict here.
- Story? Well, we know Al wants a bottle of coke and Bob is going to the store. Not really a story there, more like general events.
- Background? We might be able to guess a few things, but we

don't have much to work with.

<u>Verdict</u>- Not dialog!

Now for the second exchange...

Al: Hey man, off to the store?

Bob: (cheerful) You know it! Jenny's coming over tonight and I need to get some fixin's so I can make dinner for her.

Al: Well, I guess we know who's going to be worshiping the Porcelain God tonight! Can you grab a 2 litre of Coke for me?

Bob: You promise to be out of here by six?

Al: Scouts honor. I can't stand the sound of barfing.

Bob: I hate you.

Al: But Snuggles! I thought we had something special?

Bob: (sighs) Just be gone by six.

- Character? Bob and Al now have distinct ways of speaking, and clear personalities.
- Motivation? Bob and Al both have clear goals and desires. Bob wants a nice home-date with Jenny, and Al out of the house. Al wants Coke. (Simple, but it's still a desire.)

- Conflict? Bob wants Al out of the house, and Al wants Coke!
- Story? Bob has a hot date and needs his annoying roommate gone.
- Background? By the way they talk and interact, we're shown they know each other well, Bob isn't a good cook, and that they live together.

Everything in a story has a purpose, from the plot down to the punctuation. Nothing should be wasted. Nothing should be extra. Your car's engine doesn't need extra parts, and your story doesn't need extra bits either. Dialog in a story is no different. Every word of it has a job to do, there are no extra words. If there are, you need to get rid of them, or replace that slacker with something that pulls its weight!

Obviously, this isn't easy. As the saying goes, nothing good ever is.
When you first write dialog, it's probably going to be crap.
That's okay. Everyone's early dialog is crap!
That's what editing and revision are for. First you write crap, then you

polish it until it shines.

Practice is what lets a good scriptwriter turn even the smallest line into not only one that works hard and gets the job done, but also sounds natural and even interesting.

That's your goal- dialog that works, but doesn't sound like it's doing anything at all.

Text vs. Subtext

The Text is what's directly said.

The Subtext is what's hidden underneath those words.

For example: A girl and boy are walking together from the library and the girl says, "These books are really heavy."

The Text is: "These books are really heavy."

The Subtext is: "Help me carry these books, dummy!"

People often don't say what they mean, and neither should your characters.

You need to be aware of character goals, motivations and limitations in a scene. This will help you understand what a character can and can't do, and what strategy they will use to get what they want.

The best writing almost always contains subtext. Subtext is what keeps the audience interested by stimulating their interest and curiosity. Double-meanings, hidden humor, motivations, desires, fears, limitations- all of these are often conveyed by subtext. It's a useful tool, and an important one to master if you want to be a master storyteller.

In the previous example, the girl wants the boy to help her, but doesn't want to ask him directly because she finds it embarrassing to ask. Therefore, she uses an indirect approach to tell him that his help is needed. This tells us about her character, and perhaps even about her desires without her directly stating them. Much more interesting than the direct approach might be. (Although sometimes the direct approach can be equally entertaining, if you find an interesting way to present it.)

One note- the ability to read subtext is often strongly influenced by gender and culture. Women are generally better at dealing with subtext than men are by nature, mostly because their brain's language processing centers are bigger than men's. However, because they can read the subtext so clearly, women often forget that men aren't as attuned to it as they are.

This causes many, many, many arguments between couples.

It is also a great producer of drama and comedy, so don't let this go to waste!

How to Write Dialog Well

For many people, writing dialog is difficult, and when you're first starting out it can seem pretty intimidating.

One approach to writing dialog that often works for beginners is to use a "outline" technique. In this technique, the writer first starts with a general outline, and then slowly becomes more detailed until the scene is laid out in dialog.

This is done in steps. How many steps will vary with the writer and their approach, but generally it works like this:

1. Write a general outline of the scene explaining what happens in it.
2. Break that outline down into speakers and what generally each speaker needs to say.
3. Now turn that outline into actual rough dialog.
4. Refine that rough dialog into something more natural sounding.
5. Keep at it until the lines sound natural but still serve their purposes.

So, here's an example of the method in action.

Step One

Two men, Gregor and Boris, are arguing over the price of a fine saddle. Gregor is the buyer, and wants to get it as cheaply as possible. Boris is the seller, and he wants to get the highest price possible. The men know each other, and Gregor is trying to use their history to get Boris to lower the price, but to Boris, business is business. In the end, Gregor reluctantly buys the saddle for a higher price because he values their relationship more than the money.

Step Two

The scene starts with Gregor complaining that the price is too high. Boris counters that the quality and workmanship are fine, and that Gregor is blind if he can't see it. Gregor changes his approach, and says that Boris should give him a discount on account of their long friendship. Boris answers that their friendship is the reason the price is so low already. Is Gregor trying to cheat his old friend? Does Gregor value their past so little? He is offended. Gregor, seeing that he has hurt Boris's feelings, caves in and agrees to pay the price. Boris, seeing the effort it took, offers to take Gregor to dinner. Gregor asks why, and Boris says to celebrate a sale! It is his treat. The balance is restored.

Step Three

Gregor: It is too expensive.

Boris: This is fine Corinthian leather! And look at the workmanship! If you think the price is too high, you are a blind man.

Gregor: But, even if the quality is high, you are charging too much to an old friend. How long have we known each other? You should be nicer to someone you have a shared history with.

Boris: It is because of our history I am giving you this price! Are you trying to cheat me? Do you value our past so little you would put money before it?

Gregor: Boris, I meant no offense.

Boris: Leave. I don't want to sell it to you.

Gregor: I will buy your saddle for the price you ask.

Boris: I am not sure I want to sell it to you.

Gregor: Be reasonable and sell it to me. For old times?

Boris: For old times? Okay. Yes. For old times, I will sell you this saddle.

Gregor: Here is the money.

Boris: Thank you. Now, this work has made me hungry. Let me take you to dinner. I need to celebrate a new sale, and there is no one else I want to celebrate it with.

Not too bad. It carries the scene, but doesn't sound natural, and there isn't a strong sense of character from the two men. Also, the ending is a little flat.

Step Four

Gregor: Expensive. Expensive. You ask too much!

Boris: What? What do you mean? Can you not see this is fine Corinthian leather? And the stitching! I dare you to find a better saddle! Bah! You are a blind man!

Gregor: Maybe it is...

Boris: Of course it is!

Gregor: But, even so... How can you charge so much to an old friend? Have we not broken our bread together? Shared our nights over many a bottle? Can you not make it a bit cheaper?

Boris: What is this? Do you think I am cheating you? I am already giving you a discount because of our friendship, and now you ask for more? No! If you think money more important, then go! I don't wish to speak to you!

Gregor: Boris...I....

Boris: Leave my shop, now. I will sell you nothing!

Gregor: (sighs) Boris, be reasonable.

Boris: Oh? Am I unreasonable? Look who is talking! You are the one trying to cheat an old friend!

Gregor: I am not trying to cheat you. I am trying to buy a saddle. At...the price you ask. Please, for old times, sell it to me.

Boris: For old times?

Gregor: Yes.

Boris: At my asking price?

Gregor: (reluctantly) Yes...

Boris: This...I will do. For old times. Now, put the saddle over there and we will go to dinner.

Gregor: Go to dinner?

Boris: Yes. I have to celebrate my new sale, don't I? And who else would I do it with but my oldest friend Gregor?

Much better, they speak with different voices and in different ways. There are more lines, but those are there to convey character and make the dialog smoother and more realistic. It feels more like a real conversation. The ending is also much sharper, and more of a surprise to the audience.

Step Five

And so on...

Until you feel you've polished the dialog enough that it carries the story along and displays character and whatever else you need it to do while still sounding natural. This isn't the only way to do dialog, and depending on your skill level you might skip a step or two, or add a couple more refinement passes, but it can work.

Some people who don't feel dialog is their strong suit use this method to compensate and produce something that sounds pretty good.

It does take some extra time, but if you struggle with dialog, the results may be worth it.

Questions for Documentary Filmmakers

Most of this book is focused on narrative films telling a story, but for some of you the goal is to make a documentary instead. That's wonderful, and a lot of the things I talk about in this book are just as applicable to documentarians as they are to narrative filmmakers, especially once you get filming.

However, the way documentary filmmakers prepare to film is a little bit different than the narrative film-making process. While narrative filmmakers write scripts, film them, and then edit them, a documentary filmmaker will normally research, then film, then write a script, and then edit. The script to them is just part of the editing process, and is sometimes even skipped entirely.

That said, if you're going to make a documentary film, while you might not have a script before shooting, you do need a plan. So, before you start trying to film your documentary, you better answer these twenty-one questions in as much detail as you can.

1. What is the central question or who is the central character of your documentary?

2. Why are you choosing this topic?

3. What are you trying to achieve with this documentary? (goal/purpose)

4. Who is your intended audience?

5. What is the tone of your documentary?

6. How will the style of the documentary reflect the goal you're trying to achieve?

7. Where will you find people to interview?

8. Who are you going to interview? (minimum 3 people)

9. What questions will you ask the interviewees? (minimum 5 questions per interviewee)

10. Where will you get your information for this documentary?

11. Who will narrate your documentary?

12. What style of music will you use in this documentary?

13. Where will you get the music for this documentary?

14. What will each group member do during production?

15. How many days will this take to film?

16. How many location shoots will you need?

17. How will you get to the locations?

18. How much B-Roll will you need? *

19. What will you need B-Roll of?*

20. What photographs will you need?

21. How much will this documentary cost you to make?

*- B-Roll is video of things other than the main subject that is used to provide background, or just to make the film more visually interesting. For example, if I was doing a documentary on Canned Soup, my main subject might be interviews with the people involved in making the soup or running the factory. But, I would need B-Roll of the factory inside and outside, of the canning process, of the workers on the floor and in the offices, of the soup on store shelves, the delivery process, and so on. When making a documentary, you shoot everything and figure out what you need later, so shoot as much B-Roll as you possibly can!

Storyboarding

Storyboarding is when you take your script and basically turn it into a visual plan showing everything that's going to happen from the camera's point of view. It looks a little bit like a comic book, although usually doesn't have the word balloons and includes arrows to indicate camera motions.

If you want to save a lot of time and trouble when you actually go out to film this project, you should probably storyboard or make a shot list (Which is a bit like a storyboard, but without the images- pairing dialog with different types of camera shots.) Doing this lets you know exactly what you're going to film before you actually try to make it, and lets you map out the look of the story beforehand. It also acts as a safety net to keep you from getting confused when you're out filming and may not be doing the scenes or shots in order.

You plan out where the camera is going to be, what the focus of the shot is, where the actors will be, how the camera will move, and so on. Each time you have a different shot, you have a new image on the storyboard to represent that shot. It's very simple, and not too hard to get the basics of with a bit of work and practice.

I recommend tracking down some tutorials on Youtube, which can give a much more detailed overview of this very visual process than I can in this book. Also, most of the storyboarding programs I mention have tutorials specifically for them you can find as well.

When it comes to making storyboards, you have a few options.

<u>Oldschool</u>

The first, oldest and cheapest is to get a piece of paper, a pencil and a ruler, and then divide that piece of paper into 3, 6 or 9 boxes. Use each of those boxes to show the camera shots and movements in sequence, much like a comic book. The images in the boxes don't even have to be more than stick figures and simple lines, just so long as you can understand them and explain them to a few other people.

Slightly Less Oldschool

In this method, you use small squares of paper (or better- sticky notes!), and stick them to a bulletin board, corkboard, notebook pages, or any other surface they can be attached to. You use each square as a single panel, draw your shots out, and stick them up in order. This has the advantage of allowing you to re-order or replace shots on the fly, and is a method still used by many directors today in the entertainment industry.

Newschool

Obviously, since the advance of computers and the Internet people have created storyboarding software. There's a few programs out there like *FrameForge Pre-Viz Studio, Toon Boom Storyboard Pro, Storyboard Quick*, and *Storyboard Artist* which have 3D-characters you can manipulate (getting rid of the need to actually draw unless you want to) and lots of fancy extras like pre-rendered sets, pre-set camera options and so on to make your storyboarding experience as easy can be.

The problem with them is that they're also really expensive (*Toon Boom Storyboard Pro* is US$999 at the moment) because someone has to pay for all those features, and they're really only intended for professionals to use.

So, with that in mind, what kind of digital options do you have if you have a much (MUCH) lower budget?

Generating Storyboard Images

There are almost no programs you can get for free that have pre-rendered 3-D characters, backgrounds, or props. So the truth is, you're going to have make the images for your storyboards yourself. This can be done a few ways:

- Draw them on paper and scan them or take pictures of them.
- Draw them or composite them using a computer art program like *MS Paint, GIMP* or *Photoshop*.

- Pose your friends/relatives/actors and take pictures of them to make a "living storyboard".
- Pose your toys/dolls/action figures/models and take pictures of them.
- Generate them using free online webcomic-making software like Pixton.com or Bitstrips.com
- Generate them using free downloadable 3D computer graphics software like *DAZ Studio*.
- Make them using *Google Sketchup*, Google's free 3-D design program. (I highly recommend trying this method out. *Google Sketchup* has literally tens of thousands of free pre-made sets, characters and objects you can grab and use to create scenes to real-life scale. It's practically made for making storyboards!) Type "Google Sketchup Storyboards" into your search engine of choice and you'll find literally hundreds of tutorials and articles on the topic. It's become a very popular method of generating storyboards.

It really comes down to your taste and budget. One tip you'll find useful is knowing how to capture screen images on your computer, so that if you generate artwork on screen using a program like *Google Sketchup* you can easily save it.

To capture a screen image on a PC, hold down the CTRL key and tap the "Print Screen" key on the upper right of your keyboard. Then open your art program of choice (I usually just use *MS Paint*) and hold down the CTRL key again and hit the "V" key. Voila! An image of everything that was on your screen will appear, and you can now crop it and save it as needed.

If you have a MAC, you can either use Command-Shift-3 to take a shot of the whole screen or Command-Shift-4 to let you select an area on the screen to capture and then save it do your desktop for later use and editing.

Making Storyboards

Once you've generated your images, you'll want to put them together into a storyboard. The good news is that if you downloaded *CELTX*, you've already got storyboarding software sitting on your computer. *CELTX* not only lets you make storyboards, but they're connected with your script if it's in *CELTX* format and that's pretty handy.

If you don't like (or want) *CELTX*, there are a few open-source alternatives out there. One is *Storyboard Tools*, by Freefilmsoftware.co.uk, which is a simple but effective way to organize your storyboards quickly.

Of course, the reality is any art program or photo-manipulation program can be used to string your images together into a storyboard. You could use *MS Paint, Photoshop* (or its free alternative- *GIMP*), *FLASH*, or even non-art programs like *Powerpoint* or Word Processing software like *WORD, PAGES* or *Open Office Writer*.

In addition, if you're a Tablet or iPad user, you actually have some very good (and not too expensive) options available to you.

For iOS devices, there's *Shot Designer* (free), *Storyboarder Toolbox* ($1.99), Storyboard Composer ($14.99) and *Cinemek Storyboard Composer HD* (29.99). All are good programs which have been around for a while, and allow you to do things like photograph backgrounds with your device's camera and then manipulate them to create instant, on-the-spot storyboards.

For the Android set (who have probably been feeling left out as they read this book), there are actually even more options than iOS! You have the simple (but free!) *Storyboarder*, the more advanced *Storyboard Studio* for $5, and tablet version of *Storyboard Quick* for $20.

One more option some indie filmmakers use to storyboard is they use their video editing software of choice to assemble the storyboard. They insert the storyboard panels as images into the video editing tracks for roughly the same amount of time the actual video would be there. Also, they sometimes will actually do panning and zooming motions on the storyboard panels themselves to simulate the camera motion for the final shot.

One advantage of this approach is that you could literally just drop in the real footage to replace the storyboard images as you completed the film, so you'd know where everything goes and see it all in order. Of course, this method may take longer than the more traditional storyboarding method as well, and could easily become a whole project by itself if you start adding music, sound effects and voices. (Although, if you were looking for investors to help fund a project, you might consider doing this as a way to show them what they're investing in and give them more confidence in your abilities.)

Breakdowns

With Storyboards, you're preparing what to do with the lights and camera, with Breakdowns, you're preparing everything else. In short, you "break down" a script into all the important elements you'll need for each scene. You go through every action or description line of the script and note the following things for each scene individually:

- Characters
- Sets
- Locations
- Props
- Extras (Non-speaking actors)
- Special Crew
- Makeup/Hair
- Costumes
- Special Equipment
- Set Dressing
- Vehicles
- Special Effects
- Sound Effects

You can find template sheets to do it online, or just print out your script and sit down with a pile of different colored highlighters or pencil crayons and pick a color for each type of item. Highlight or underline each item in each scene in the same color for easy reference, and then use that for making a list of who and what is needed for filming each scene.

Of course, if you're using *CELTX* to write your script, all you have to do is highlight each item and then add it to the Master Catalog by using the Breakdown list tab on the right side of the screen. (Look for the icon that looks like a little Tablet or mobile-phone to open up the breakdown options.) As you highlight each item and add them to the Master Catalog, it will let you fill in lots of details and notes about each thing and character. Then, you can use the Reports Window (check the tabs at the bottom) to print off (or make PDFs of) sheets with lists of everything needed in each scene or the whole script. It's really very convenient once you get used to it.

Breakdowns are one of those things that seem skip-able until you get out to your filming location and discover you left half of what you'll need at home, which is two hours away and you need to film now! Don't be lazy, do a breakdown, it will save you a lot of time and trouble in end.

Budgeting

Now, you might be thinking "Budgeting? Would be nice to have a budget at all!" And, if you don't have one, that's why you're borrowing everything and relying on favors to get things done.

However, even doing it as cheaply as possible, it's very likely you're going to have to spend a little money at some point. It might be on equipment, it might be on transportation, it might be on paper or printing for posters, or (most likely) it might be on food and drinks for yourself and your actors. But it will likely happen, so you better be prepared for it.

My suggestion, if you can, is to have at least a little money as a "production fund" set aside and available in case you need it. You might not tell anyone it's there, but having it there will make you feel a lot more secure in case it's needed. It doesn't matter if it's just $20 to cover Pizza and Pop, or $100 to $200 to cover light bulbs, extension cords, a hat, gas and coffee, but try to think ahead about what might cost you money and set something aside to prepare for it.

In the end, if you don't end up using the money, then you can use it for something else! (Maybe put towards your next film project!) But, not being broke if/when money is needed can sometimes make or break your production.

Costuming/Makeup

In Indie film-making, it's best to have the actors take care of their own costumes and make-up, unless it's really specialized. (Like monster makeup, special effects or wounds.) However, you should be prepared to let them know exactly what they'll need. (Why Breakdowns are important!)

Remember that for continuity's sake, the characters need to have the same clothes, hair and makeup in each shot, or it won't all fit together later in editing. Make sure that you maintain that consistency, because otherwise you're looking at reshoots or having to do editing tricks to try to work around something that would have taken almost no effort to fix during filming.

Be prepared to provide lights, mirrors and places for the actors to change or do their makeup, even if it's just the back of an SUV or a nearby washroom you scouted out earlier.

Props

Finding the right props can make all the difference in selling what we see on the screen, but it can be hard to do on a budget. Here's a list of a few places to hunt for props and costumes for your no-budget film:

- Dollar stores
- Thrift stores
- Pawn shops
- Auctions
- Your Grandparent's House

- Yard sales
- Garage sales
- Car Boot Sales (aka Boot Fairs) in the UK
- Goodwill/Charity stores
- E-bay
- Kijiji
- Craigslist

Remember, the first rule is that film-making is about illusions. You need something that looks like it could be the item you need on screen, what it actually is doesn't matter! The only thing that matters is what the audience thinks it is when they see it!

Scouting Locations

Next to finding actors, locations are the trickiest part of pre-production. If you made a proper Rodriguez List and worked with the locations you have available, things might not be difficult at all, but if you were feeling ambitious and wanted to push things a little, you might now have to find a few new places to film.

The first rule of locations in film-making is to remember that everything we see on camera is what the director wants us to see. What does this mean? It means that since we can control what the audience sees, we can trick them into seeing things that aren't really there.

A simple hallway in a local community center can be a hall in a school, an office hallway, a hall in a military base, or even part of an underground bunker system where the last survivors of humanity are hold-up against the zombie hordes. It can become any of these with a few simple set decorations like potted plants, fake signs stuck to the walls or doors, and colored lighting. The only limit is your creativity and ability to scrounge set decorations.

So, when you scout locations for you to film in, always look for not just what's there, but what a place can become with a little work. Of course, it's always better to have a real hall in an office building to film in for authenticity, but since you have no budget you have to work with what you have available and where will be convenient to film.

Speaking of which, as I mentioned in the Equipment section, remember that if you're using your Mobile Phones to film you can do it pretty much anywhere and most people will ignore you. Yes, you can't bring any lighting equipment with you or they will get suspicious, but if you rehearse ahead of time (and then are quick enough) you can film almost anywhere. Scenes can be done at local restaurants with good lighting (sit near the window, or use outdoor cafes), on busses and trains, in stores and malls, and even at amusement parks or tourist attractions.

Another tip is to be aware of local festivals or events and plan accordingly. If your local school is having a street fair and you need a fair as a background, slip in and film! Many cities have special festivals in the summertime, and you can use these to get amazing backgrounds for your scenes that would cost thousands of dollars to stage!

Of course, never do anything dangerous, illegal or immoral, but since you can't afford permits, you have to make the best of what public spaces you can find. Also, be aware of local parks and beaches and what they have to offer- sand dunes at the local beach can become a distant desert country with a few choice angles, and wooded parks can be medieval forest kingdoms. Watch out for cool backdrops like waterfalls, mountains or dams as well!

One last thought to keep in mind- with selective editing you can make things appear where they aren't. Footage taken at a huge sporting event can be combined with footage taken in your community center gym to to make it look like a huge audience is watching your characters play basketball! People entering a concert hall can be made to look like they're coming to see your lead character's new concert. Just because we see your characters walk into a mega-million dollar office tower, it doesn't mean the actual interior shots take place inside that building at all!

Again, the only limit is your own creativity.

Finding Actors

The truth is, most indie filmmakers use their friends, relatives, classmates and co-workers as their actors. Sometimes this works well, sometimes it doesn't, but often you work with what you got.

One thing to keep in mind when considering roles is that film is a visual medium, and while someone might be a terrible actor when they open their mouth, they could still be useful as long as they can show basic emotions. There are whole movies where some or all of the characters don't say a word, but convey everything in body language.

Your Dad might sound awkward while trying to say lines, but if you ask him to cross his arms and shake his head, the idea of "no" can be conveyed just as clearly. Remind him how he felt when you asked him for $1000 to help make this film, and I'm sure he'll find the proper emotional state!

A speaking role that can be converted into a silent role frees up your better actors to take the roles that can't be silent, and gives you more flexibility in your casting. (It also lets your friends and family who want to be in your film, but can't act to save their lives, still participate and feel they got their big chance to be on the screen.)

However, sometimes you have more actors than you have roles, or perhaps you don't have enough, and have decided to throw out a wider net.

In that case, it's time to do some casting.

Casting isn't an easy process, but it's not a complex one either. Here's the normal method for holding open auditions:

1. You pick a place.
2. You set one, two, or more times when you'll be doing casting.
3. Set up a website.

4. You announce that place and time to anyone who's interested.

5. The people who are interested show up, and you meet with them one by one, having each of them read a sample of the script.

6. When you're done, if you're still not sure you call the ones you think were interesting back to read again.

7. Inform everyone of your decisions.

See? Simple.

Let's go through each of these in a little more detail. (Of course, only use the steps or parts which apply to you, which not all might.)

1. Pick a place.

It's important to choose a place to cast where the actors will feel comfortable, and where you will have a little bit of privacy with them. You don't want the actors to feel more nervous than they already are, and you need a place where you and your assistants are alone with them while other actors can wait nearby for their turn.

Generally, unless you're only casting friends and relatives, try to avoid using a house as a place to cast. Asking people to go into a stranger's home isn't going to make them more comfortable, and you might lose some potential actors when they find out it's a house because it looks unprofessional.

Ideally, you need a semi-public place with two separate rooms- a place for people to wait, and a place to hold the auditions. Your best bet for these would be asking if you can use space at a school, a local library, a local community center, a church, or maybe even a real office if you know someone who might let you use the space. In a pinch, in good weather, you could use an outdoor space like a park or garden, but the problem is still that you need a way to separate the candidates from each other for a time while having some privacy.

2. Set one, two, or more times when you'll be doing casting.

If you're holding open auditions, where you're advertising and just seeing who's interested, then you may want to have more than one audition time (and maybe place as well). Not everyone can make every time because of personal commitments, and even if you pick times when people are more likely to be free (like evenings and weekends) some people just won't be able to make it. So, since you don't want to miss potential actors, if it's possible hold your auditions more than once.

3. Set up a website.

While not required, we live in a digital world, so I recommend putting up a website first, even if it's just a free blog on Wordpress.com or a Facebook page, and posting...

• General information about the project

• A list of the roles being cast, noting the gender, age range, and any other important details of each character in one sentence or less.

• Short script samples to go with each role (for the actors to study their roles and lines before the auditions)

• Your contact information

• Dates and times of the auditions

• Anything else you think the actors should know

This will again make your project look more professional, and it gives them somewhere to check and find more information about the project. It also makes your life a whole lot easier, since you can just post the link online instead of having to repeat all your casting information everywhere you go to advertise.

4. You announce that place and time to anyone who's interested.

This is another important step- you need to let the world know that you're looking for people to star in your amazing project. At a local level, you might try making a poster and sticking it up at schools (especially places that have drama classes), community centers, libraries, stores, or anyplace else with a bulletin board. If you want to cast a little wider, then you could also announce it on places like Craigslist, Kijiji, Facebook, Twitter, Reddit (there are subreddits for almost everywhere), Local acting bulletin boards, Local newspaper and community websites, and anyplace else you think local actors might see it.

Now, just to save everyone a lot of trouble, if this project involves no money and only pays in experience and credit, then just be honest with your actors right up front during the advertising phase. Write "Unpaid" on the announcement and be done with it. If you try to bring in actors who want pay and then they find out the truth, they'll just feel unhappy and walk away anyway. By doing it like this, the people who show up know what they're getting into and everyone can feel a lot more comfortable with the process. Yes, you'll only likely attract amateur actors, but then they might still be a lot better than your cousin.

5. The people who are interested show up, and you meet with them one by one, while having them read a sample of the script.

On the assigned day and time, show up at the meeting place very early, and if possible put up a sign or something to let people know this the place for the auditions. (You don't want your actors getting confused.) You may also want another sign asking them to take a seat and wait until they're called if you don't have someone else standing outside to act as a greeter.

Speaking of other people, if at all possible, you shouldn't be meeting with these candidates alone. There's the safety issue (especially if you're young or female), but just as important is having a second (or third) opinion. Have someone else whose opinion you trust there to give you feedback on the actors, it can make a world of difference to have your thoughts confirmed, and they might notice things you don't.

So, once you're ready, have each candidate come by themselves and give a self-introduction. Introduce yourselves as well, and chat for a minute or two to make them comfortable, and then when you're ready have them read the lines you've prepared. (Print off copies of the script samples to take with you so that actors can use them, even if they're also online.) Be prepared to have you or one of the other judges read the lines for any characters other than the actor. Don't feel you have to act, though, just read the lines and let them be the ones who show off acting ability.

You should also be recording these auditions, in either video or audio for later review in case you need to check them again to make a decision. Then, once they've gone through the lines once, ask them to read the lines in a different way to test their ability to take direction and their ability to show different emotions or styles.

After you're satisfied, thank them for their interest and coming, and tell them you'll let them know once you've made your decision. Also, tell them the date you plan to make the announcement or if you plan to make all decisions that day you could even ask them to wait if possible. If you're doing it another day, make sure you have their contact information before they leave!

6. When you're done, if you're still not sure you call the ones you think were interesting back to read again.

This step depends on whether you have more than one person you're considering for a role or not. (A very common situation.) If you do, then have them come back and read for the role you're considering, but this time try bringing them back in pairs. Have them read opposite to one of the other candidates for that same role or another role so that you can see the dynamic between them and how they act and react with another actor.

7. Inform everyone of your decisions.

Discuss, consider, debate and do whatever you need to do to decide who you want to play which roles, and once you do- let them know. Don't forget to also contact the people who you didn't choose as well, and let them know as gently but honestly as possible. Tell them that after discussing it with your fellow judges you decided that the other character fit the role better, and do your best to reassure them that you still appreciate them coming and trying out. Encourage them to try for another role if you do this again, and that you hope you can work together again in the future.

Keep in mind, if something happens with the actor you did choose, you might still need to be able to come back to this person and ask if they're still interested later!

Table Readings

Once you have your cast and crew assembled, a good idea is to do what's called a Table Reading. This is where everyone meets in one place and reads over the script together. It can be your living room, at a restaurant, in a lunchroom, or anywhere else that can fit all of you.

For the actors, it's a chance to meet the people they'll be working with and start to see how the whole project will come together. It's also a chance to ask you (the director) questions about the script, their characters, and how you want them to play the role. (So be prepared!)

For the crew, it's a chance to figure out who will do what, and what will be needed for the production. Since they too will see the story as a whole, and be able to look at the storyboards and breakdowns (if you have them), they can see what their roles will be and ask questions from you about what you'll need each of them to do.

In addition, for you, the Table Reading will be your chance to see and hear the script being read by your actors for the first time so that you can start to visualize the movie as it will play out with them. It's also a chance to revise your script to suit the people you've chosen, or even alter some of the casting based on who might suit one role better than another.

Finally, it's your chance to make sure everyone knows their place, so that when the actual filming happens you don't have to worry about telling each person where they go and what to do- they'll know it already. This is especially important in indie productions because the actors need to know what clothes to wear or makeup to put on, and the crew need to know what they need to bring from home.

Also, sadly, this is also your chance to see how reliable people are going to be. Since you're working with volunteers, their enthusiasm and dedication will vary a lot, and some people who say they'll help might not turn out to be all that helpful. (Or turn out at all!) If people can't even spare the time to do a Table Reading (without a good reason), then how can you expect them to show up for actual filming?

If people don't show up for the table reading, you don't have to fire them immediately, but you might want to have a "Plan B" in case they don't show up to filming as well. A good General always plans for the unexpected, and so should you! Doing this will let you know where some of the problems might pop up, and then you can start thinking about how to deal with them.

Chapter Three: Filming

Getting the Most Out of Your Phone's Camera

Always shoot in landscape mode.

Your TV screen is horizontal, your monitor is horizontal, and any video you take on your phone should be as well! It gives you more to edit and play with, and unless you purposely want to shoot vertical for a Found Footage look, there is no benefit to filming that way.

Many people hold their phones with one hand, and this is fine for some still pictures, but with video the results will be pretty shaky unless you have really steady hands. Using Two hands will add much more stability and decrease shaking as long as you tuck your elbows against your sides and move your body not your arms to turn the camera.

But there is another way.

Hold the camera in one hand, but hold it so your fingers are facing out and the screen is facing toward you. Make sure you fingers aren't blocking the camera lens (which should be at the upper left of the mobile) and then flatten your upper arm against your side like so...

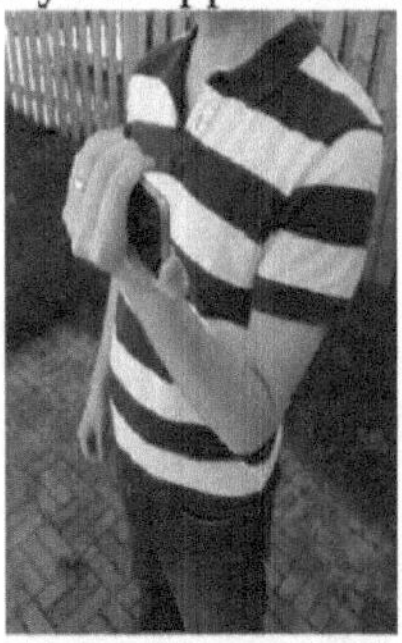

This position is the natural one for your arm, so it will cut down on the shaking and make things much more stable overall. Just remember to move your body, not your arm when you want to move the camera- keep your arm locked in that position. This will make your phone much more stable while you're standing still, but will only help a bit when walking or running.

Other Rules:

Always Turn On Airplane Mode

- Before filming with a phone camera make sure you put the Phone into Airplane Mode so nobody can call you.
- Incoming calls will stop your recording, and can generate noise and other problems in audio recordings.
- It makes your battery last a long longer because your phone isn't searching for wifi or connecting to the local mobile tower grid.

Empty Your Phone First

- On an iPhone your memory is limited and precious.
- Back up your phone on your computer or iCloud and then erase all of your music, podcasts, pictures, and whatever else is taking up room.
- You can always re-install them from backups later.
- Remember- 4-5 mins at 1080p is 1GB in Filmic Pro!

Charge up your Battery

- Video software is a power hog.
- Make sure you have a fully charged battery before you start shooting.
- Bring along a way to recharge your phone like a laptop or extra batteries.

Clean your Lenses

- Before you shoot, make sure you clean your lenses.
- Have a tissue or dry lens cleaning cloth handy in case dust gets on the lens.

Bring Extra Phones

- Having more than one phone is an advantage, so use it!

- Also, make sure you have more than one Phone with your filming software installed on it so that you can take multiple angles at the same time or switch primary cameras if there's an issue.

Camera Controls

There are three very basic things you need to be able to do on a (mobile phone) camera to get the best video from it-

- Set White Balance
- Set Exposure
- Set Focus

Your phone does all three of these things automatically, but you should learn how to control these functions yourself if you want to use your phone to film quality video.

Why Not Just Let the Phone Do It?

Mobile phone cameras are designed to be used by pretty much everyone, regardless of actual skill at photography. The problem is that camera phone software is still pretty dumb. One shake the wrong way or one shadow can cause it to change the settings and ruin your takes. The basic software is also calibrated for still photography, not video, which was a bit of an afterthought, so you can't expect it to take great video.

Set White Balance

Simply put, setting White Balance is a way to teach your camera how to interpret different colors in your scene. You show it what White looks like, and it uses that as a baseline to figure out what all the other colors look like under those lighting conditions as well. This is important because it will help determine how sharp and clear your colors are.

Setting White Balance on your phone is super-easy, and it just needs to be set once at the start of filming the scene. (Unless you change the lighting setup or you're outside filming for a long time.)

1. Stick something white (like a piece of paper or the back of a white t-shirt) at the spot where your actors will be standing.
2. Focus on them and lock your White Balance on your software.
3. Congrats! All done! Step complete!

You should know the iPhone automatically tends to shoot "Warm", which means it will naturally give the video a slightly orange-ish color. On the other hand, Android cameras will tend to film "Cool", so they will have more blue.

This means the footage from the two types of cameras won't always match up in color temperature. Don't worry about it. You can easily fix this later using video editing software like *Premiere* or *Final Cut Pro*, but don't be surprised if you suddenly find the colors don't match when you try to mix raw footage from the two phone types.

Set Exposure

Exposure on a mobile phone camera is basically your camera trying to balance how light or dark the image is. If you point the camera at something bright, it will let in less light and darken the image to compensate. If you point the camera somewhere dark, the phone will brighten the image by letting in more light.

When you set Focus, you should also set Exposure at the same time. Do this by putting your Exposure Reticle on the Subject and then tap Lock Exposure at the bottom of the screen so it turns red. (If you're using Filmic Pro, or other software that allows for a separate exposure reticle) Some software and cameras only has a single reticle for both exposure and focus, which is fine, make sure you lock them on the subject so they don't change.

If you've done this, now you don't have to worry about it suddenly changing on you while filming because it decided to focus on a dark spot or light spot.

Set Focus

Naturally, you want the subject of your pictures to be in focus, nothing is worse than a blurry/unclear image. Your phone will automatically try to maintain focus on whatever you put the focus reticle on, and will set it's focal distance for you. But, the problem is that if you accidentally move that reticle over something farther or closer away, it will change focus on you to that new thing, putting your subject out of focus. (This is especially an issue if your target is moving, or if you have shaky hands.)

iPhones also have an incredibly annoying quirk when it comes to video called "Chasing Focus"- when they decide on a new point of focus they actually go out of focus on everything for a split second and then refocus on that new point. This can literally kill shots, because often it's not something you can remove easily in post and looks awful. (It should be noted that Android phones don't do this, they just refocus on the new subject without going completely out of focus first.)

Locking Focus is your best and simplest weapon against this problem. Have your subject(s) stand where they will be for the shot, lock focus on them, and you're good to go.

Moving Targets

Once your focus is locked, you can't change it and if your actors move they risk going out of focus. That means that if you have actors or camera people moving in a shot you only have a few choices:

- Make sure your actors don't move around much during shots.
- Take many short shots instead of trying for long ones.
- Move with the actors.
- Have a focus "zone" that the actors move into and out of.
- Risk autofocus, but stay close enough to your actors that there's no chance of you focusing on something besides them.
- Risk autofocus, but plan to cut around any focusing issues.

The Importance of Blocking

"Blocking", or doing a practice run through where everywhere will stand or move before filming a scene, is extremely important with mobile phones because it lets you set your Focus, Exposure and White Balance for the final scene.

You can't change locked focus during the scene like you can with a more professional grade camera. (At least, not without risking the automatic features ruining your shots.) So, make sure you rehearse and set all of those things beforehand if you want consistently good shots from your phone camera.

Use pieces of tape on the floor/ground to set marks where actors need to stand or stop during a scene, that way they'll be at the right spots in perfect focus.

Other Important Controls

When you're shooting with multiple cameras, always make sure all cameras are shooting at the same resolution and frame rate. (This is important at the editing stage.)

I recommend shooting at 1920x1080 resolution. (Don't use the iFrame option unless you're specifically shooting for a Mac editing program.) 1280x720 resolution is fine if you really need to save space on your camera/card, but don't go lower if you can avoid it.

For frame rate, 24 frames per second, 25fps or 30fps are all fine, just pick one of them and stick with it, don't jump between different frame rates! (24fps will save a little space, but not a significant amount.)

Digital Zoom

Digital Zoom is just a fancy way of saying that your camera is making the picture bigger.

It looks like it's getting larger (zooming in) but in reality you're just zooming in on a small part of a big picture. You're actually losing picture quality, because the image isn't getting bigger, it's tricking you into thinking it is.

In short, don't use it. You can simulate it in editing with less loss of image quality anyways.

Lighting

The word Photograph is made up of two latin words- *Photo* meaning "Light", and *Graph* meaning "Writing". So, to create a Photograph is to literally write with light.

There is no more important element in photography than lighting.

Lighting can literally make or break your shot or your scene- learn to do it well, or else!

Part of the reason for this is because even the best cameras aren't as good as the human eye at dealing with light. The camera sensors need more light than people do to process an image, so what looks good or okay to us often isn't enough light to produce a high quality image, especially on a phone camera.

You usually need multiple, bright lights to properly light a scene, or the sun, which is literally the universal light source for taking video.

<u>Shooting Indoors</u>

If you'll be shooting indoors, you'll generally need at least 3 sources of light to light up your scene, and this is called a 3-Point Lighting Setup. There are other kinds, but if you can master this one you'll be able to shoot your videos properly.

A 3-Point Lighting Setup consists of a Key Light, a Fill Light, and a Back Light (also called a Head Light or Rim Light). The Key Light is the brightest of the three, and is usually placed between 15 and 45 degrees to the right or left of the camera. The Fill Light is there to fill in the shadows created by the Key Light, and is usually half the brightness and placed on the opposite side of the camera from the Key Light. Finally, the Back Light is usually behind and above the subject and pointing down on their head so that it creates a rim of light around their head and shoulders to separate them from the background.

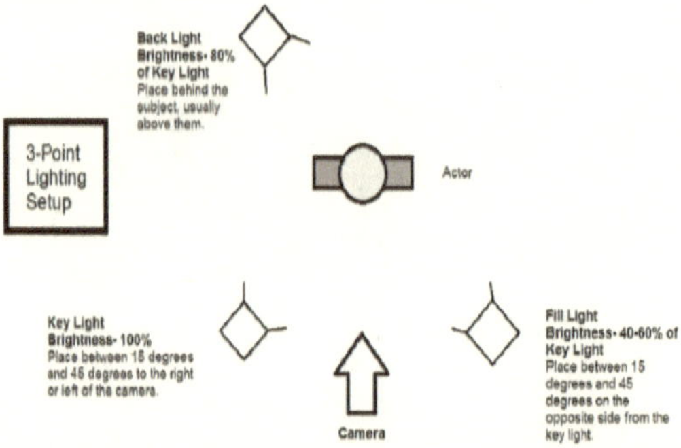

Since it's often difficult for zero-budget indie filmmakers to have a proper elevated Back Light, there is an alternative- a Background Light. A Background Light is different than a Back Light because it's focused on some Background elements instead of on the Subject. It's another way to separate the subject from the background, and is the more flexible way to do it. Almost any light behind the subject can be used as a Background light- a hallway light, a lamp, or even light reflecting off a wall. Just so long as it gives you a way to separate the subject from the background, it's good.

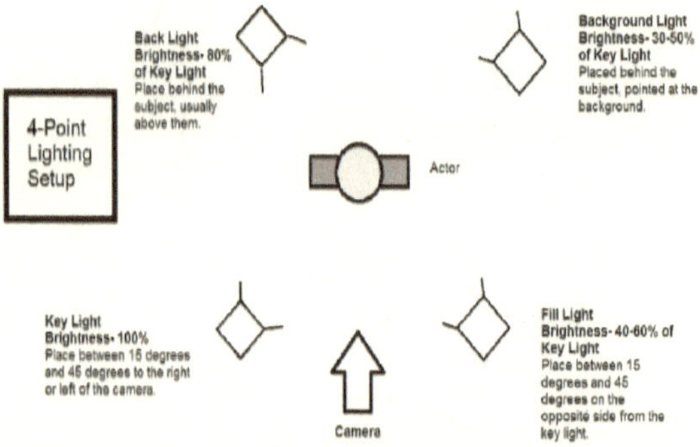

By the way, if you have a setup with a Key Light, Fill Light, Back Light and Background light, this is called a 4-Point Lighting Setup. (See, you've just learned two basic setups in one!)

If you're going to use Floor Lamps as a cheap and easy light source, I suggest using the following method: Stick the tallest and brightest of the lights just off camera to the right or left of the camera to act as the Key Light. Then, stick a second floor lamp on the opposite side, but put it twice as far away as the first one so it can act as a Fill Light. Finally, if you have a third lamp, stick it in the background behind the subject(s), preferably next to a wall so the light reflects off the wall and acts as a Background Light. Try to make sure it isn't too bright or close, it shouldn't be more than half the brightness of the Key Light.

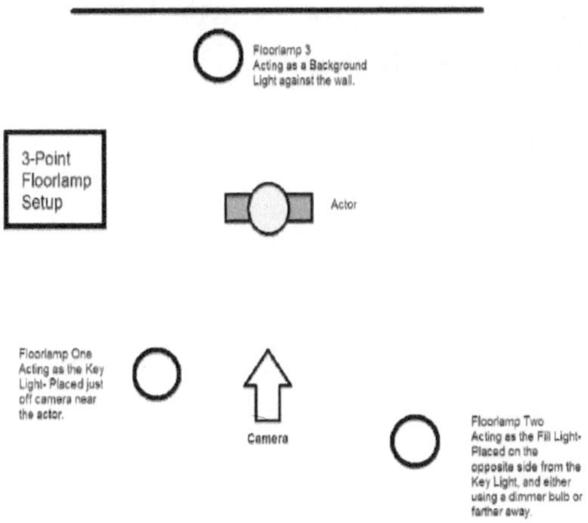

Of course, the 3-Point Lighting Setup is just the beginning, a starting point in understanding lighting. But, let me emphasize again that lighting is important to how your scene will look, especially on a phone camera. Learning how to light a scene properly can let you coax some amazing results even from camera phones.

Basic Lighting Tips

- Use the brightest light source in the area as your Key light.
- Don't position your subject with their back to a very bright light, especially a window on a sunny day!
- Even low-quality lights can be used as a Background Light- like light spilling in from a hallway or reflecting off a wall.
- Try to control the light in a room, and remove light sources you don't need to avoid unwanted reflections or shadows.
- Avoid shooting subjects which have very bright and very dark parts, because the camera sensor will have trouble dealing with the extreme contrast and it can ruin your shot. (Especially if you're using auto-contrast.)

Outdoor Lighting- Working with the Sun

The Sun is the best source of light for photography, but it's harder to work with than most people realize. You have to plan and watch carefully when working with the sun as your Key Light, because so many things can affect it.

You want to shoot for visual consistency, so the light matches in all your shots. It makes them easier to edit together, but the problem is that sunlight changes color depending on the cloud cover and the time of day.

As the Earth spins, the color of the light changes due to:

- The time of day.
- The angle of the sun.
- The atmosphere.
- The amount of atmosphere the light passes through.
- The composition of the atmosphere.
- Cloud cover.

This means the White Balance of your shots is changing on you, and that video taken at different times of day on different days sometimes won't match in light and color. You can often fix this in editing, but not always so be careful. Sometimes it's better to try again another day.

- Direct Sunlight is also often too bright and will result in overexposure
- Filming in mid-day (10am-3pm) on a Sunny day risks overexposure and really harsh shadows if the subjects are out in the Direct Sunlight. During these times film indoors or under shade.
- The best time for filming on a Sunny day is the early morning or late afternoon/early evening. The Sun is also at a better angle for filming- you want the Sun to be a Key Light, not a Back Light.
- Photographers call the hours after Dawn and before Sunset the "Golden Hours" because the strength, color and angle of the light is perfect for photography. So be ready to take advantage of this!

<u>Shooting on Cloudy Days</u>

On a Sunny day, a cloud passing in front of the Sun can be a poorly-timed nightmare. It cuts off the light and changes its color, and all you can do is wait for it to pass. (Snack break!)

However, a cloudy but dry gray day (especially one with high, light cloud cover) is your best friend in the world. It gives you soft, diffuse light that is perfect for filming, especially in mid-day when the sun would normally be too bright. Even if it's just a little dark, you can use the Sun as the Fill Light and have another Key Light, or brighten it in editing.

Shooting in Low-Light/Night

One major problem mobile phone cameras have is that they are not very predictable at low-light conditions. If you're in an urban environment with lots of lights around, the results can vary from poor to surprisingly good. (But you absolutely need to lock White Balance and Exposure!) But, if you're in a low-light environment without a lot of lights around, like a campfire or suburb, the quality probably won't be very good at all.

This leaves you with a few options:

- Avoid shooting at night/low light.
- Stick to brightly lit areas like downtown streets.
- Use the newest phone possible. (Newer phones handle low light better.)
- Bring in your own lights to improve quality.
- Shoot Day-for-Night.

B.Y.O.L.

The trickiest part of night shooting is powering your lights. Where to find power sources?

Lights strong enough for filming use a lot of power and go through batteries quick, at best portable batteries will likely only give you 2-3 hours of filming time.

You can also use a gas generator, but it will make a lot of noise and can only be used when you're capturing video, but not audio. You have to stick in the audio later, or do the scene twice- once with poor light but no noise, and once with the noise and then match the good audio with the good video in editing.

Day-for-Night

Day for Night is when you film during the day, and then make it look like night in editing. It can also be done while filming, depending on the camera or software.

The basic rules to make it work are...

- Film on a cloudy day to avoid sun/shadows.
- Avoid showing the sky in your shots. (Although you can chroma-key a pure bright blue sky.)
- Watch out for reflections on windows, etc.

Sound

"If it sounds good, it looks good."

This is a Hollywood mantra which should also be engraved in the heads of everyone who wants to shoot a film of any kind. It doesn't matter if it's a narrative film or a documentary, nothing will turn an audience off from watching your film faster than bad audio.

People will watch films with poor video quality if the sound is good, but if the audio is bad they won't even last a minute. So, you need to make sure that even if you don't have Hollywood-level video, your audio sounds as good as you can possibly make it.

And, as I mentioned already in the Gear section, the best audio is going to come from external recorders designed to capture sound. But, what if all you've got to make your whole production is a couple of smartphones?

You're in luck, because that may be exactly what you need!

Things to Know

Mobile phones are designed to capture fairly good quality audio and send it winging off through the airwaves, so they're fine for recording sound for your movie too- provided that you keep a few simple things in mind:

- Mobile phone mics are designed to be short ranged, because they're supposed to be focusing on the owner's voice and not the ambient noise around them. The makers of Smartphones assume their owners will be walking through crowded urban areas while talking on them, and design accordingly.
- Mobile phone mics are directional, so they're designed to pick up sound in a cone shaped pattern out from the bottom of the phone. (Where the owner's mouth is most likely to be found, if they're human.)
- Mobile phone mics are mono, since the designers assumed that

nobody needs stereo sound during a normal phone conversation.

If you remember these things, and plan accordingly, you can then start to use them to capture sound for your film. There's also a few simple tricks you can do to greatly improve your sound quality:

<u>Trick One: Doubleshot</u>

For this trick, you simply film your scene twice, once in close-up, and once farther away at whatever distance you want the majority of the scene to be at. Then, when you edit the scene you use the close-up audio (which has the better quality) with the farther away footage. Ta-dah! You have the sound quality of being close up, but you have the distance away from the actors you want for the scene. You also have two sets of distances you can jump between in editing to make the scene more interesting visually.

One minor thing to remember, though, is that both takes need to have almost identical delivery by the actors, otherwise the close-up sound won't match up with the footage from farther away.

When doing this, I also recommend using an elastic to attach a credit card or some other card to your phone to make your sound more directional.

<u>Trick Two: Multi-Phone Recording</u>

Generally, the best recording will almost always be done not by the Camera Mic, but by a separate Mic located on or near the actors or subjects. Since most filmmakers have more than one phone available to them, you simply record video with one phone and audio with another, and then join them together in post production.

It works great outdoors, and it's even better indoors!

You can place the phones on the actor's bodies to function as Mics, and use things like the Earbud Mic on the Apple earbud set's volume control as a mini-lapel Mic to hide on the actors and get better quality audio. I've also experimented with just placing my iPhone upside-down (with the Mic facing up at me) in my shirt's breast pocket with pretty good results.

You might need to use two or more phones to record, and then mix all the audio sources together in Post-Production, but that's still a huge improvement over the sound you might get otherwise from your filming phone, and produces totally usable results.

<u>Trick Three: Hidden Phone</u>

One last trick you can use is to hide the additional phone being used to record audio somewhere on the set near the actors with the Mic pointed up and towards the actors. Say, if you have two people at a table and then slip the phone behind a box of tissues, salt shakers, or a picture so that it can pick up the sound while remaining hidden. Of course, since it's in contact with the table it may also pick up vibrations from the actors touching the table, so put it on a padded surface to absorb the vibrations.

Extra Trick!

To save yourself a huge amount of time in editing, make a loud noise each time you start filming like clapping your hands or ringing a bell. This will show up on the sound editor as a big spike which is easy to see, that way if you need to mix in audio from multiple sources you can just line them all up on the time-line before you start editing and removing what audio or video you don't need.

Now, the truth is all of these tricks probably aren't going to produce sound as good as a decent Lavalier or Boom Mic will, but if you can't afford to buy something like that, this can make a big difference.

Basic Camera Shots

There are many different kinds of "shots", which is the term for the way in which the camera views the subject(s) on the screen. You're probably familiar with at least some of them, but it's good to have a common way to describe different shots and know what effect each has. Keep in mind, there is disagreement about what exactly these terms mean, and there are many different variations and combinations.

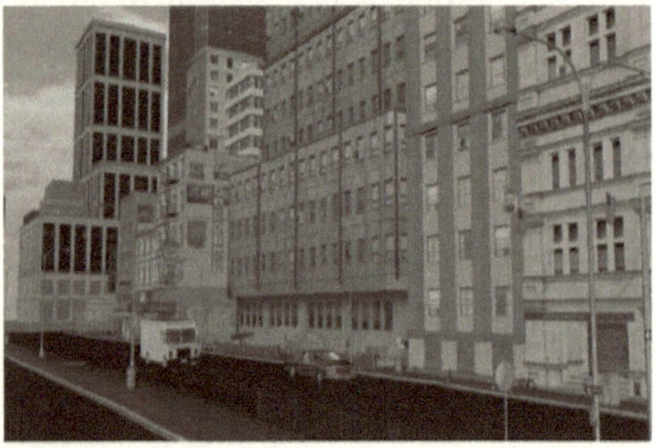

Extreme Wide Shot

This shot looks out over a landscape or large area, and the subject of the shot will be tiny at best. (If they appear at all.) This type of shot is best used as an Establishing Shot, a shot which tells us where something takes place and gives us a sense of a place or environment.

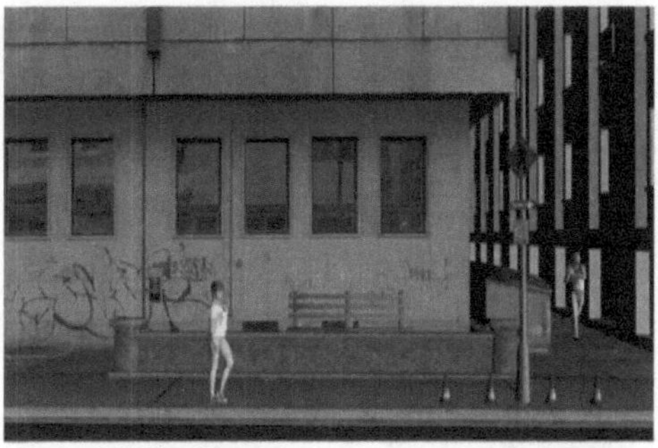

Very Wide Shot

A shot where the subject is just a small presence, but clearly visible and which gives us a strong sense of where the subject is placed in an environment. Wide shots where the character is alone can make them look isolated, or if they're surrounded by people it gives us a sense of their part in the group.

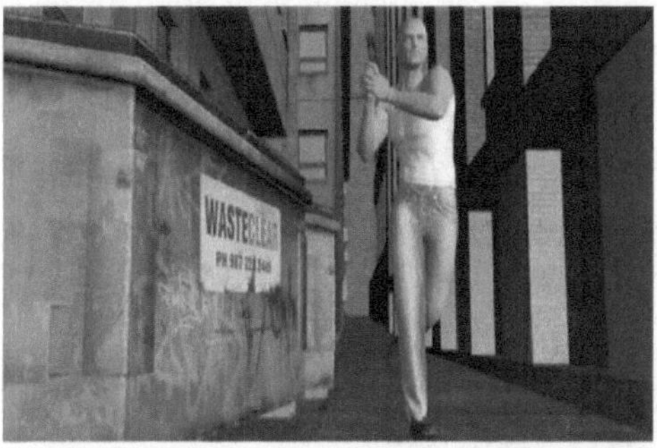

Wide Shot (aka Long Shot or Full Shot)

In this shot, the we see all of the main character (or subject) and we also get a sense of the environment around them. Generally, the subject will fill the screen from top to bottom, or close to it.

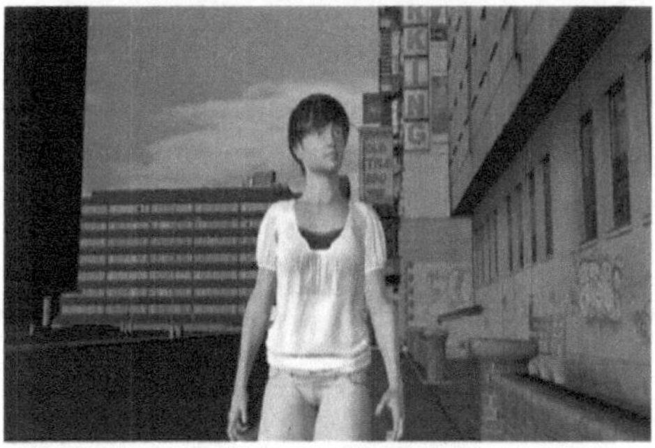

Medium Shot (aka Mid Shot)

We see the subject/character from approximately the waist up while still getting some sense of the environment around them. This is how people look to us when we're talking to them, so this is a relaxed and casual position. We can see emotions and body language easily on them, but it's not intense. Most news interviewers we see on TV are in medium shot.

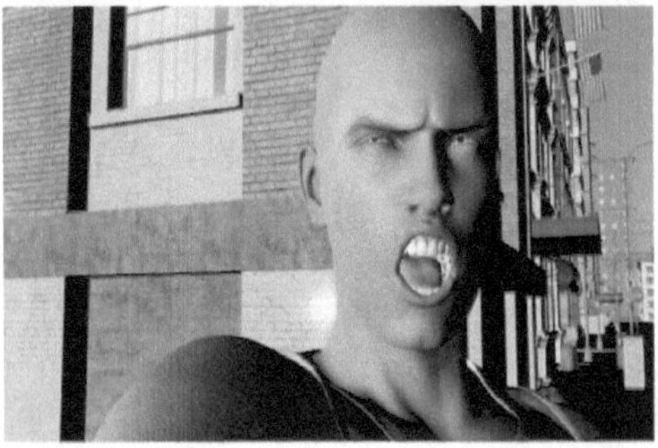

Close-Up

A large part of the subject takes up the whole frame, often the head of a character, but it can be other body parts. This type of shot pulls us into the subject's personal space, and emphasizes emotion. We can see any emotions they feel in detail, and it lets us seem to feel what they feel.

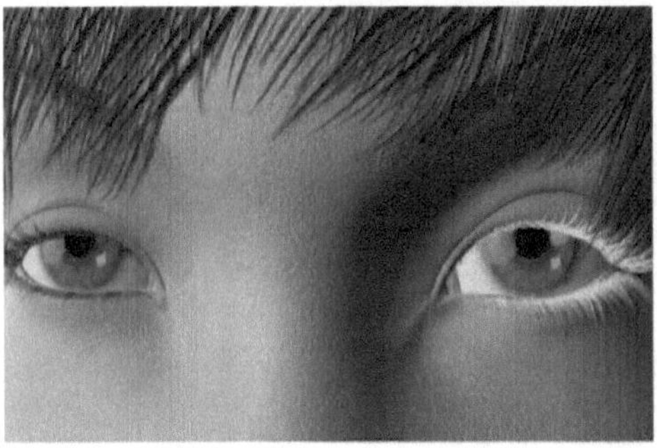

Extreme Close-Up

The camera is zoomed in on some small part of the subject's body so that this small part takes up the majority of the image, like just the eyes, a fingernail, a nose or mouth. We're actually too close in for anything but the most extreme emotions, so the emphasis here is on details.

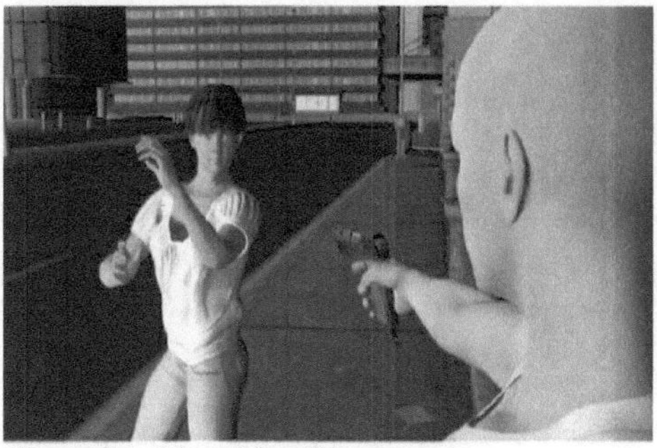

Over the Shoulder Shot

We're looking over the shoulder of one person at the person or thing that they're facing. The closer person's head should occupy no more than 1/3 of the frame, to the right or left side, with the real subject of the shot being on the vertical thirds line of the other side. Very common in dialog scenes, but remember the 180 degree rule!

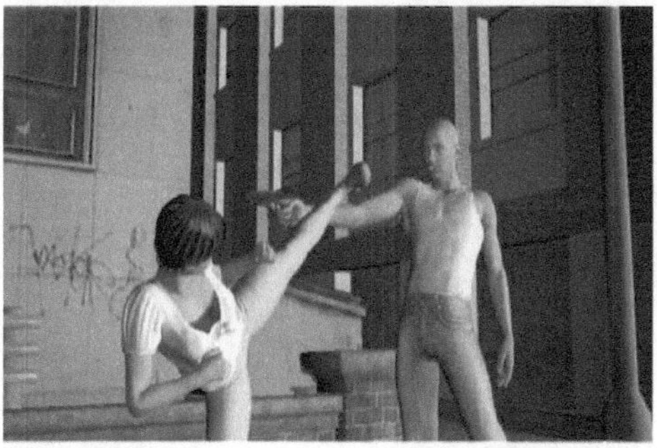

Two-Shot

A shot with 2 people in the frame, usually a Medium Shot with them next to each other, but it can also be a Wide Shot. If both are at Rule of Thirds intersection points, it indicates both have equal importance. If only one is at an intersection, it tells the viewer that this person is the focus while the other person is less important.

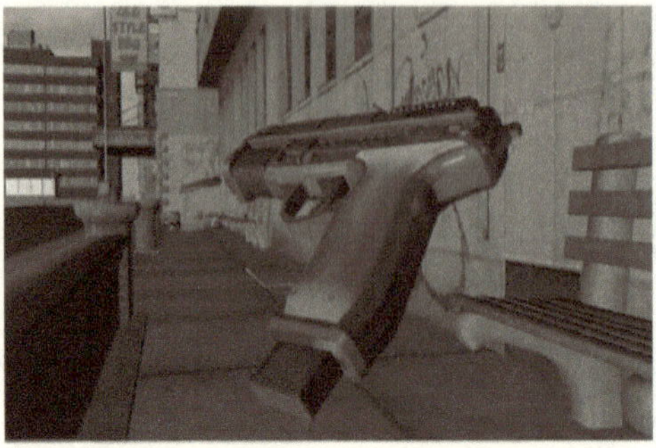

Cut Away

A shot of something other than the subject of the main subject. Sometimes used to provide emphasis, to stretch time, or to build tension.

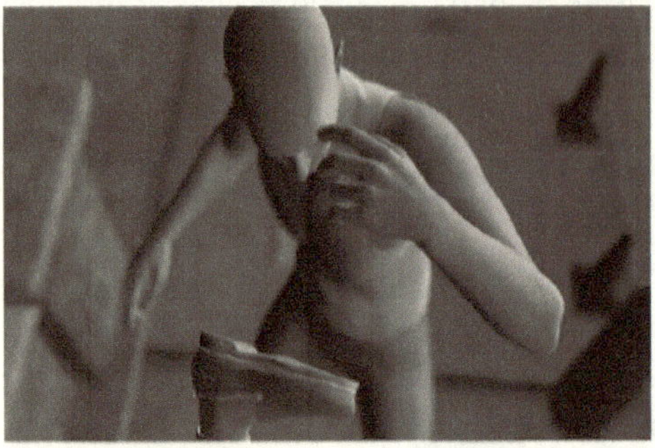

High Angle Shot

A shot looking down on the subject. It makes the subject look small and weak.

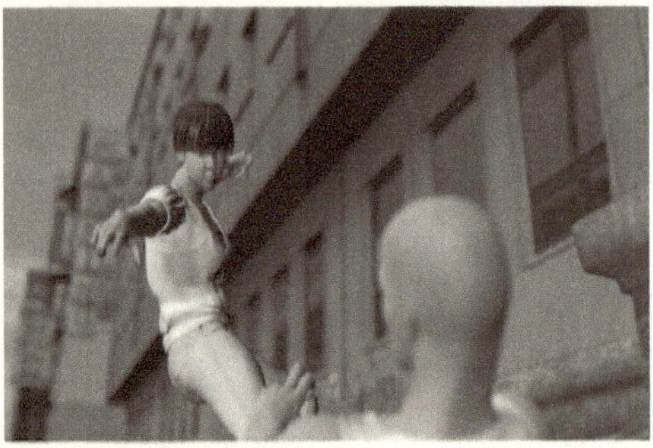

Low-Angle Shot

A shot looking up at the subject. It makes the subject look large and strong.

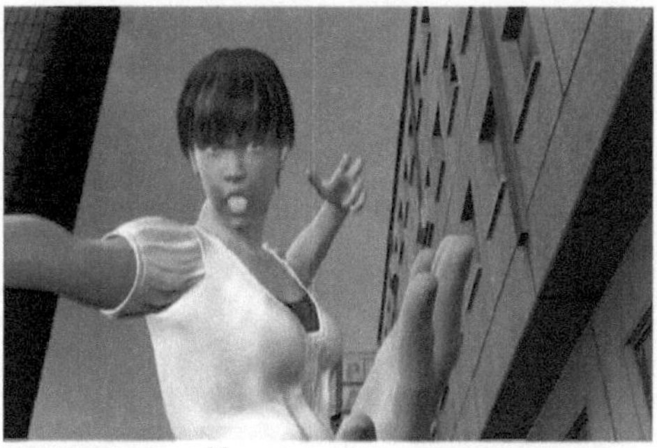

Perspective Shot

A shot in which we're supposed to be looking from the eyes of a character or subject. It should follow a setup shot that lets us know whose eyes we're looking out from if possible.

Master Shots

A Master Shot is a special kind of shot, usually a Medium Shot or a Wide Shot, which shows the events of the whole scene and everyone in it from beginning to end. It is important to get a Master Shot of most scenes (usually as the first takes you film) because once you have a good Master Shot you have a usable version of the whole scene. No matter what happens from that point on, you have the scene done, and even if there was a fire alarm or the weather turned, you could use that shot in your film to tell the story.

In addition, there is another important reason to get a good Master Shot-editing. Usually the Master Shot is followed by more takes from different angles (such as the Triangle Coverage method we'll discuss in a moment) and when you go into editing you can use the Master Shot as the starting version of the scene upon which you layer and edit other shots and angles onto make it more interesting.

So, always make sure you get a good Master Shot of the scene first! Then get fancy after that, knowing that you've covered the basics you need to put that scene of your story on film.

Triangle Coverage

Let's face it- most movies are about people (or giant robots, or vampires that look and act like people), and the core of movies is about those people interacting with other people. This means that you're going to have to film many situations where you have two people actually talking to each other face to face.

There are many ways to film this, but if you want to be able to really play with it in editing later on, you'll probably want to use what's called "Triangle Coverage". With this method, you film the scene (at least) three times, each from a different camera angle, like this...

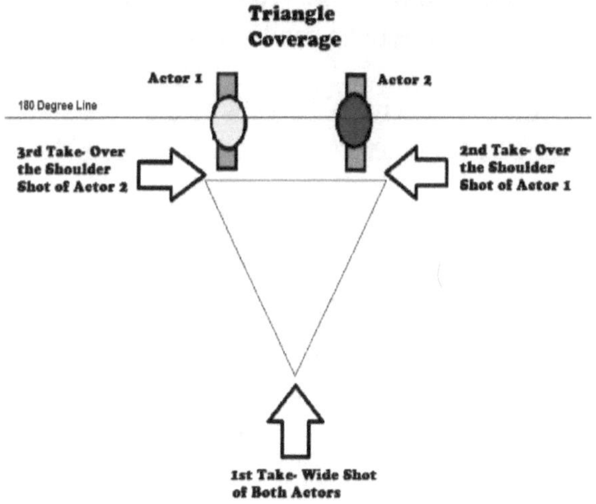

As you can see, the arrangement looks like a triangle, which is where the name comes from.

The main reason to do this is to give you the best possible options when filming the scene. It gives you a lot more control of the scene when you get into editing, and lets the scene be a lot more dynamic and interesting. A single medium two-shot of two people talking doesn't give you a lot to work with, but being able to cut between different angles will make your scene much more lively.

It also lets you film a scene using a single camera and using the same lighting setup. (Which is a huge advantage for Indie filmmakers.) You simply movie the camera and lights between takes, and it creates the illusion that you have several cameras and a large lighting kit even when you don't. (Bonus!)

Notes on Triangle Coverage

- Make sure your actors don't speak over each other. (Have them pause a beat between each line.) This allows you to edit between them more easily.
- If you have more than one camera, you can speed things up by filming more than one "point" at the same time, but make sure the other cameras aren't blocking light, casting shadows or just getting in the way.
- You can change the lighting for each angle, but make sure the lighting matches up or it will look odd.
- If you can, think about how you want to edit your scene before you shoot it. If not, take shots of everything and figure it out after.

- Don't forget to film any inserts. (Close ups on objects or actions that can later be inserted into the scene to make it seem more dynamic.)

180 Degree Rule

Simply put, the 180 Degree Rule says that once you establish a spacial left-right relationship between two actors you stick to it! If you establish Bob on the Left and Jake on the Right, you stick to that arrangement until you tell the audience that the locations have changed with a new Wide Shot.

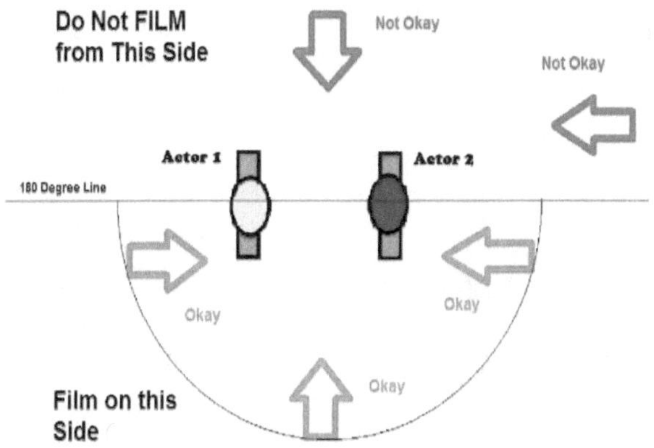

The 180 Degree Rule is important because you must never break the 2nd Commandment of film-making- "Thall Shalt Not Confuse Thy Audience"

If you say Bob is on the Right and Jake is on the left and then show them on different sides in single shots the audience loses track of the scene and is busy trying to figure out where they are instead of paying attention to your story.

Notes:

- This rule still applies when you have 3 or more people in a scene, but is based on the 180 degree line between two characters (or two groups of characters) who are speaking to each other any any given time.
- The 180 degree line can actually change within a single scene, but make sure you let the audience know things have changed with a new wide shot to show new locations.

Rule of Thirds

The Rule of Thirds is perhaps one of the most important basic rules of film-making, and will be one of the very first things any photographer or cinematographer is taught to master. It's one of those things that's been in front of you your whole life in almost everything you watch, but you won't notice it until it's pointed out to you.

It's also one of the things that separates amateur video from something better, and just using it will up the quality of your images.

So, what is it?

In short, any image can be divided into 9 squares, and we use these squares to arrange that image so that it looks and feels balanced. Things positioned in the middle of the screen feel isolated to the viewer, but things placed slightly to the left or right of the screen allow the viewer to feel that there is a world around that subject.

Here's some examples.

First, here's a basic Rule of Thirds grid, this grid can change shape depending on the shape of the image, but it always divides the image into nine equal squares.

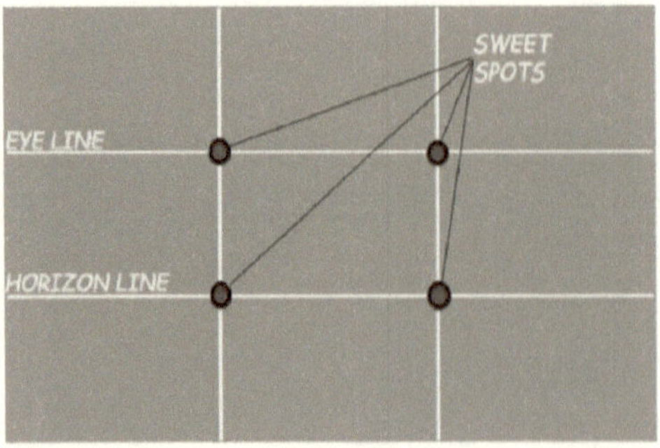

Now, here's an example of what I mentioned above. Notice the character in the middle of the image below feels isolated, and our eye looks at her, but not much else.

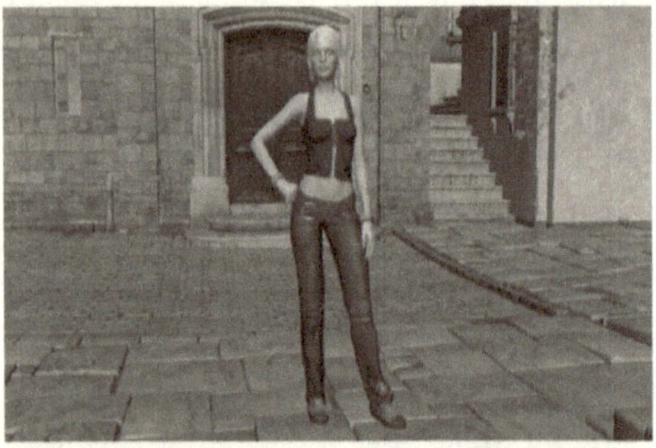

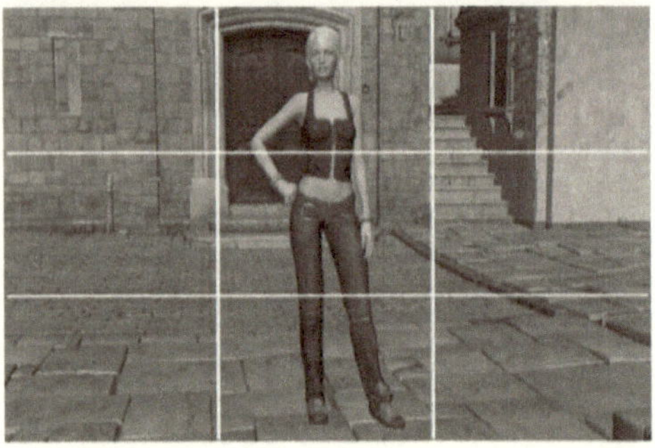

Here's the same image, but now we've moved the character into one of the "sweet spots" to allow the image more room to "breathe". Now your eye looks at the character, but then naturally starts to also look around the rest of the image at the other elements.

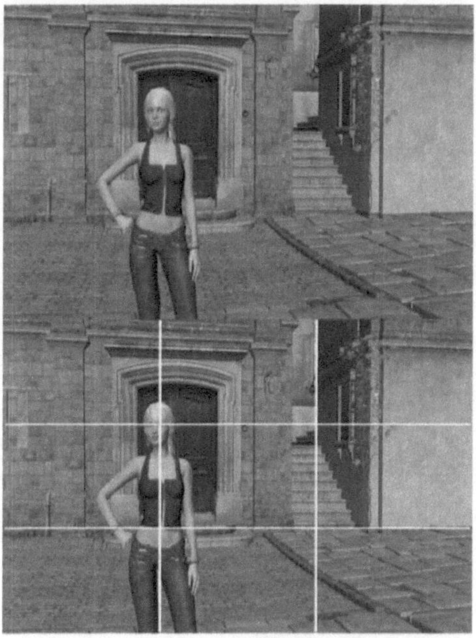

How to use the Rule of Thirds in video:

- Try to position anything important to the scene at one of the four junction points or with the lines on their center mass.

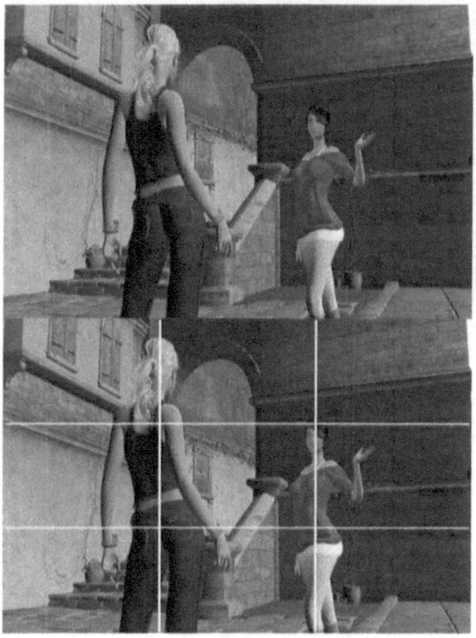

- Try to keep the focal character's eyes at the Eye Line. Also, try to keep the horizon at the Horizon Line, but if you have to choose between the Eye Line and the Horizon Line, always choose the Eye Line.

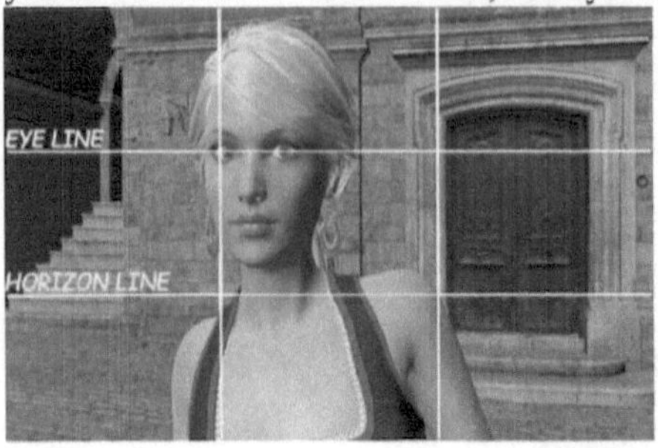

- If you have two characters in a scene, try to put them each at a junction point or thirds lines if you want the audience to focus on both.

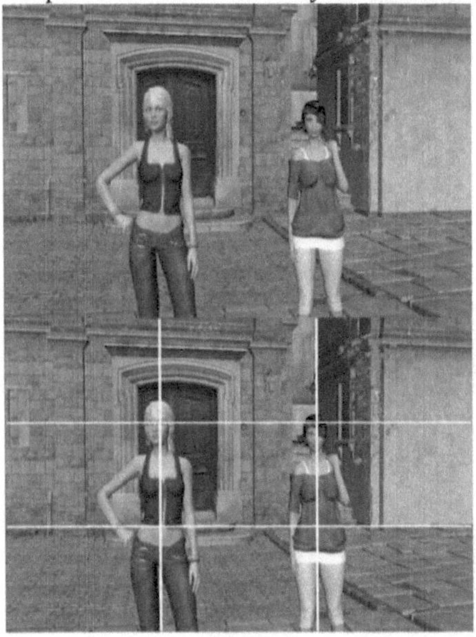

- If you don't want the audience to focus on one of them, put the less important character in the right or left third but not on the line. The audience instinctively knows that the character not at the thirds point is the less important of the two from years of watching films and TV. Think about it- which character in the image below below does your eye naturally go to?

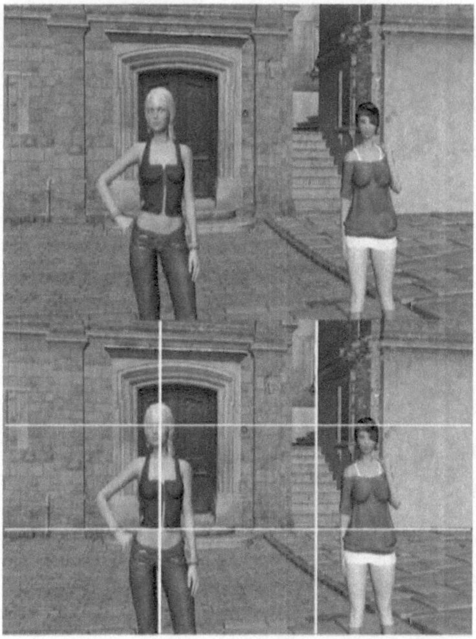

- If you have an Over the Shoulder shot, put the closer character's head in the right or left third of the screen. This tells the audience they're not the focus and frames the real focal character.

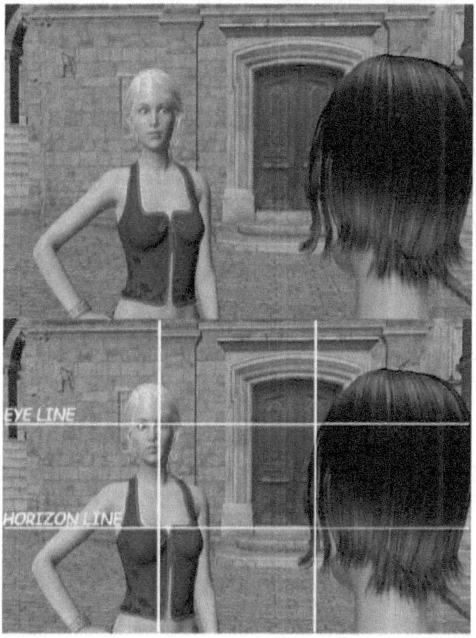

- Finally, if your shot is following a moving character in a tracking shot, keep them in the middle are as much as possible and don't let them cross into the two side zones. That will leave too much or too little space between them and the edge.

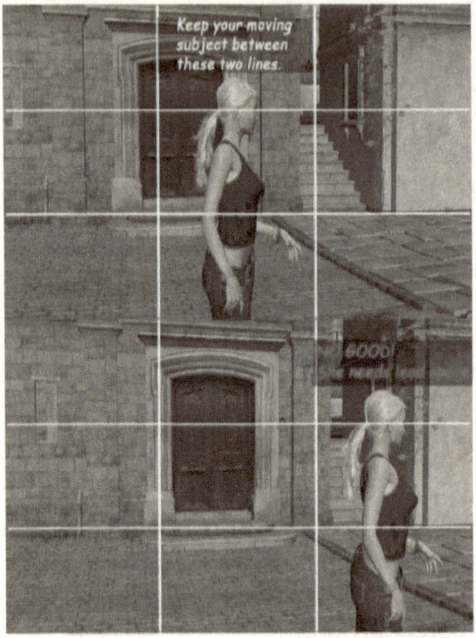

Tripod Tricks to get Better Results

Here's a few tripod tricks that you can use to make your life easier and improve the quality of your video.

Sideways Tripod Steadycam (aka The Merricam)

Modify one leg of your tripod so it can point straight out at a 90 degree angle from the shaft and then lift the tripod by that leg so its hanging on its side. You put the camera on the tripod head, and then use the other two legs as counterweights for your camera.

The theory here is that as you walk, the balanced camera won't be as affected by your body movement and it will give you a more steady moving shot. Unfortunately, this will only work on tripods that have screws attaching the legs instead of bolts (like most cheaper ones do), and it works better with heavier tripods than lighter ones.

You can also do a variant of this trick by suspending the tripod from a rope or cloth at a balanced midpoint. I've done it using my tripod's carrying bag and it works- sort of. It's still a bit jerky because my tripod is too light. It would work great for a front-back shot simulating an animal's point of view, though.

This trick often takes a bit of practice to make work, so play with it a bit to see if you can find a way to have it work for you. You can carry it with the tripod facing left-right or forward-back, and each can be used to produce different visual effects.

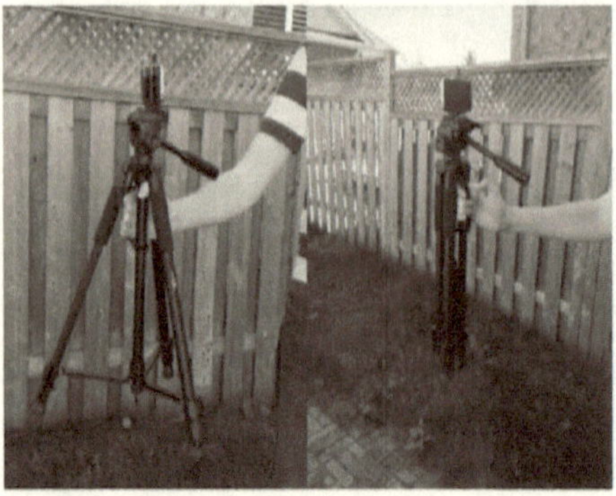

Upright Tripod Steadycam

There are two ways to do this trick, both of which will reduce the shake as you move with the camera.

1) Put the tripod's legs out, and lift it up by the middle shaft so that the distributed weight makes your camera less shaky.

2) If your tripod has a handle, leave the legs together and hold it lightly by the handle using the weight of the tripod to help stabilize your camera as you move.

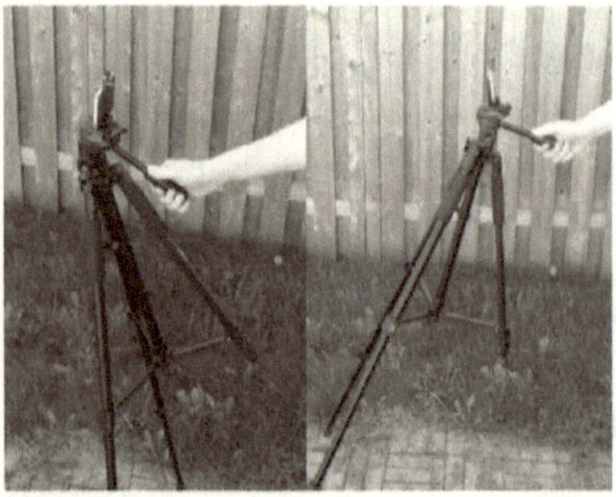

The Dolly/Bipod Trick

With this trick, you shorten one of the legs of your tripod and set it so the two longer legs are at the front side-by side. You also need to loosen your panning and tilting fasteners so that they're fairly loose.

Now you can move the camera forward or backward smoothly while keeping it fairly level by balancing it on the two legs. It won't let you move back or forward very far, but it will be enough to to add a little simple dolly-type motion to some of your shots.

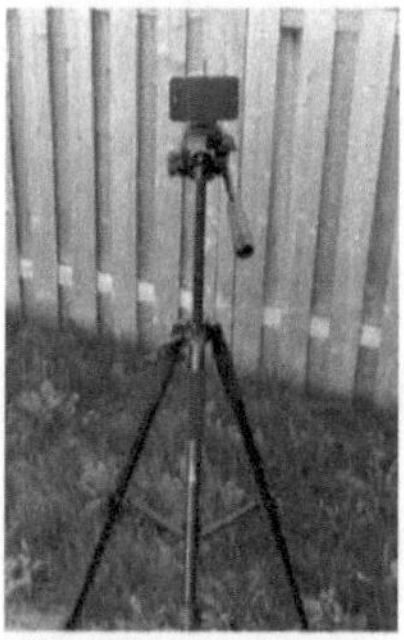

The Turtle Crane

Most tripods have a central shaft that can be cranked up or down to make the camera higher or lower. If you do this while filming, this creates a crane effect that can let you smoothly move the camera up or down to reveal or hide subjects. (Like rising over the edge of a desk, or going from over a table to showing us what's happening under the table.)

The Sliding Camera

This trick works best on smooth floors, but it can be made to work on low carpet as well. With this trick, you put something under each of the three feet of the tripod that let you slide it around smoothly. On a smooth floor, pieces of cloth might work, or pieces of cardboard that have a smooth side. The cardboard might also work on carpet, or you can also get some furniture sliders from a store meant to go under the feet of heavy pieces of furniture.

In theory, you could also do this trick on ice, but I wouldn't advise it unless you really wanted to risk your camera!

String Tripod

A super-simple and cheap trick that is as old as cameras. With this one, you attach a string to your camera with a screw or by tying it around the middle of the phone. Then you tie the other end to something solid you can step on like a washer, place it on the ground and step on it, pulling the string tight so that the tension keeps your camera from moving. This can reduce shakiness and keep your camera steady if you like holding it with both hands.

Another variant of this is to use a shorter string and attach it to a weight that gives your camera a solid downward pull. The weight will act as a steadying force to also keep your camera a little more steady. This version can be done with anything that weighs at least double what your camera weighs like bags, equipment, or even buckets of water or apples! (Not a long-term solution, but it could work in a pinch!)

Feeding your Cast and Crew

Filming is not a quick process, and it's normal for crews and actors to be working 14-16 hours a day when producing a film. As a result, people are going to need/want food and drinks, and you better be prepared to give it to them if you want a happy cast and crew. (Often the only perk to participating in a film shoot is getting "free" food- which means the producer (you) is paying for it.)

If you're just filming for an afternoon or two with your friends or family members, this might not be an issue, but it is something you should think about. At the very least, you probably want to go to your local supermarket and buy a case of bottled water (24 small bottles are often only $4-$6) for people to drink while they work and some little snack-packs of dried fruit or nuts for people to eat. (Avoid high-sugar snacks and soda pop, because it gives a quick sugar high and then a swift drop in energy levels afterward. This is especially bad for actors who need to keep their energy levels up.)

If you are running over into mealtimes, you probably want to think about how to feed these people. You could ask them to bring their own food in advance, but generally since they're already doing you a favor the least you can do is feed them. This can be pizza and fried chicken if you can't cook, or if you can then you might try making some casseroles or other dishes that can sit a little while. (Remember to keep the food cool (or hot), as food poisoning will also end your filming really quick too!)Healthy food is always better than junk food, and will result in happier and more energized actors here as well. So if you have a healthy, balanced option, always try to provide it. Save the junk for for the wrap party!

Directing Actors

Actors are not puppets waiting to have their strings pulled, they are thinking, sensitive and creative people who can often be your greatest resource when making a film. When possible, try to make the actors part of the creative process and help them to understand why you're taking the shots you are- they might even have some good suggestions you hadn't thought of!

That said, remember that you are in charge, and you're the final decider on what happens. If you don't have time to discuss why you're shooting a scene a certain way, or you don't agree with what the actor has to say, then smile and ask them to just do it this way until you get the shot you want, and then if there's extra time offer to try it their way.

Also, since you're often going to be working with completely amateur actors, remember that they're going to be very nervous and need quite a bit of encouragement. Don't lie, but try to be positive in what you say to them, and balance any criticism with compliments to keep their spirits up. It's very easy for them to become discouraged, and it can often be your job to help them believe in themselves.

Chapter Four: After Filming

Who's Afraid of Editing?

For some people, editing can be a pretty scary process. You look at that long list of video clips in the folder on your hard-drive and you think there's no way you're going to be able to turn that into anything but an awful mess. Even worse- you have a whole cast and crew who are now counting on you to turn all their freely given hard work into something they're proud of!

Talk about pressure!

Suddenly doing anything and everything but editing will start to look pretty good. All those chores you hate, your homework, or even that toilet that needs scrubbing will look pretty good. And then there's that list of films you've been meaning to watch, and TV series you want to catch up on...

Stop!

Just stop.

First- breath. Take a deep breath and let it out slowly. Do that a few more times, and it will calm you down.

Next, I want you to do the following exercise: Grab a piece of paper and a pen or pencil, and then take the words below and turn them into a short paragraph of 2 or 3 sentences. It doesn't matter if you use some of them more than once, and you'll need to add punctuation and possibly change them for tense, but try not to add any words unless you really need to.

All walk he when away in looked we would world a house our yawned on roll spends of around ran sofa if lying his time scratched my just saw home floor to laziest over hope once is and came it the at I dog then couple cat think burglar belly go have wants for and

Take a minute, put your sentences together.

I'll wait.

.

.

.

All done?

Good. Now, how hard was that?

Did you struggle with where to put the words? Or did it flow pretty naturally and everything slowly clicked into place? Did you survey everything and then plan out your sentences, or did you just start grabbing words and tossing them together?

Either way, thanks to your knowledge of English grammar, you looked at all those random bits and were able to make meaning of them. You took all of those pieces and turned them into a single paragraph which fits together pretty well and conveys a message.

Congrats, you're an editor!

What you just did with words is no different than what you're going to do with those video clips and your editing software. You're going to take out the bits that you feel work best together and combine them in such a way to convey a message to your audience. Your message might be "my garden is beautiful", or "love conquers all" or "giant robots kick butt!", but you're capable of putting it together.

All you need to do is get your butt in the editing chair and try.

The Basic Editing Process

Editing, some will say, is where the real magic of film-making happens. It is when the film is being edited that what is now a folder filled with video and audio clips get turned into an actual film. Editing is often the longest part of the whole process, and can either be the most creative or the most grueling part (or both!) depending on how you feel about it.

To edit, you will some Video Editing Software like I talked about in the Software section, a computer to do the editing on (preferably something fast with lots of free memory on the Hard Drive) and all of the video clips you've collected. You will likely also want some music files, and possibly some sound effects files as well, depending on your needs.

Once you have all that together, you can begin.

Pre-Editing

The first thing you need to do (if you haven't already) is to organize your video clips. My suggestion to you is to organize them by scene, in proper script order, creating a separate folder for each scene and putting all the clips related to that scene into the folder. You can also put any incidental music, sound effects, or other clips related to the scene in that folder as well to keep it all organized. This will make your life much easier, because you likely filmed the scenes out of order, and now everything is easier to find and already organized for editing.

Once you've done that, you want to sit down and review all of the video you've taken at least once, going through it scene by scene in script order. This will both give you an overview of the footage you've taken, and it will also let you subconsciously start to see an extremely rough version of the film play out.

As you're doing it, have a pad of paper and pen (or maybe a program like *WORD, PAGES* or *WordPad*) open, and take notes about what you see. Make notes about the shots that look the most useful for telling the story, the ones that catch your attention, and things that come to you as you watch the video. Note what files those shots are in and what time they start and finish in the clip, as this will make them much easier to find and grab when you're deep into the editing process.

Editing

Once you have everything noted and organized, you're ready to start editing. Note: Editing methods are as different as people, and each editor has their own style, so what I'm about to tell you may or may not be the best way for you to do things. It's how I would go about editing, and you can try following it, but you should also feel free to experiment and try to find what works best for you.

My method for editing would be as follows:

1. I would go back to the very first scene, and start editing from there in script order- from the first scene to the last scene, one at a time. I'd do this because if I jumped around in my editing, I wouldn't have a sense of the tone and pacing of the scenes that came before the one I was working on at the time. It would let me go through the story similar to how the viewer would experience it, and give me a solid sense of how the story is playing out. Also, it would let me spot anything that might be missing, which is easy to overlook when you're jumping around from scene to scene in random order.
2. As I started each scene, I would review all of the video clips in that folder at least twice to make sure I had a sense of what I had to work with. After that, I would put the Master Shot into the video timeline to act as my base, and begin working through the scene in order, adding clips, subtracting clips, and playing with the footage to get what I thought seemed like a good general telling of the story. If I didn't have a Master Shot, I'd begin by inserting whatever rough shots I thought fit together to tell the story in the most basic and straightforward way possible.
3. Once I had a rough cut of the complete scene that I was somewhat happy with, I'd begin refining it. An insert there, a trim here, a new shot to replace an old one- one little edit at a time I'd be working away on the scene. This is the point where the magic really happens, as you

customize the scene to how you feel it should play out. You're setting tone, you're making moments shorter or longer, you're playing with the pacing and rhythm of the scene like a musician.

4. Speaking of music, at some point in the refinement process, you're probably going to want to slip the music in there. When this happens will depend on you, and how important the music is to your scene. If it's crucial the scene and music match up exactly, and you're using pre-made music, then you probably want to mix the music in there fairly early in the refinement process so that it influences and guides your editing. However, if the music isn't so important, or if you plan to make custom music to go with the scene after it's done, you can wait until much later to add it.
5. Sound effects are similar to music- if you have important key sound effects that are a major part of the scene, put them in early to help guide your editing choices. Otherwise, add additional sounds later on when your scene is finished so you know exactly what sounds you need. (No point hunting for, or recording, sounds that you don't end up using in the final edit!)
6. Special effects would come once I'd finished the scene to what I thought was close to my final cut. Even then, I might not put more than basic or rough effects on the scene unless I was sure nothing would change later.
7. Once I've finished a scene to my satisfaction, I'd save it (and back it up somewhere off my computer, like an external HD or on the Cloud!), make a final render of it, and then move on to the next scene. I'd continue doing this until I had completed all the scenes, resisting the temptation to try and assemble them all together unless I had a special reason for it like I was putting together a larger sequence.
8. Only after all the scenes were done would I create a new master edit, load all the renders of the completed scenes in, and then watch the whole thing through from start to finish. Again, I would make notes as I watched, but I wouldn't edit anything until I'd watched it through and seen what it looked and felt like in this rough cut.
9. Now the overall project revision would begin- with me going back in and re-editing scenes again to fit better with the project as a whole. Some scenes might be fine on their own, but too long or short when compared with what's next to them. There might be extra information, or

information missing that I have to add or cut. There may even be whole scenes that need to be moved, removed, or replaced because they don't work in the greater context of the film.

10. Once the scenes are re-edited into a greater whole, I'd re-watch the whole project as a whole again and make another round of revisions until I was happy with it. At some point I'd also add transitions between the scenes, and at the very end go back and do things like final special effects, titles and anything else that needed to be done.

If that sounds like a lot of work, it is. This is why I said it was the longest part of the project, because even a short film of just a few minutes long can have several scenes in it, and each needs to be edited on their own first. The longer the film, the more editing time is needed to get the best results, and feature films can take months or years with whole teams of editors working together to craft them.

Of course, the amount of editing you put into your project is up to you, and will be decided by your goals and schedule. A very rough rule of thumb for editing is expect it to take at least two hours of editing time to fully edit one minute of screen time. If you're not familiar with the software, this can easily double to a four hours per minute or longer. If you're a fast editor, or the work isn't complex, it might even drop down to one hour per minute or less, but it depends on the type of editing you're doing.

Also, you need to understand that this Two Hours per Minute Rule is likely just for that single scene. You may still need to account for more time to edit the whole thing again once you get to the whole-project revision stage! So plan your time wisely! Your short 15 minute film will likely take you at least 30 hours to put together, but could easily be more!

Playing with Audio

While most Video Editing programs such as *Premiere* and *Final Cut* allow for some audio editing as well as video editing, there are some things than an actual audio editing program like *Adobe Audition* or *Audacity* can do much better than a Video Editor can.

The most basic and important of these is Noise Removal- Audio Editing software has special features that allow you to remove background noise from recording and just leave the parts of the sound you want. This is very useful when dealing with mobile phone recordings because the microphones will often end up picking up background noise that you'll want to get rid of to make the voices clearer.

A warning, however, if you take away too much of the background noise you'll also take away some of the depth of the voices in the process, which will leave the voices sounding hollow and strange. The best way to use noise removal is like peeling an onion- don't try to take all the noise away at once, but peel it away in small layers until you get what you want. If you look up "[your audio editor name] noise removal tutorial" on YouTube you will find many visual tutorials to help you with the finer parts of the process, and I recommend watching at least one before you try doing noise removal yourself.

Another use for Audio Editing programs is creating sound effects. While you can find many sources of sound effects online, sometimes you will need to make your own, and this often requires mixing several different effects together to produce something new. (For example, the space fighters in Star Wars are a mix of car engines and household appliances with audio effects applied to them to create the noises you year.) Sound Design is its own whole field, but just layering some basic sounds together and playing with them can produce amazing results.

Finally, one last tip for playing with audio- try to equalize all the sound to an average of -12 dB (decibels) and never let it go over 0 dB if you can avoid it. Anything over zero will produce distortion and noise, and is too loud, while -12dB is perfect for listening on most speakers.

Chapter Five: Resources

Stuff Worth Watching

YouTube Channels

Film Riot- http://www.youtube.com/show/filmriot
The Frugal Filmmaker-
http://www.youtube.com/user/thefrugalfilmmaker
Indie Mogul- http://www.youtube.com/user/indymogul
Indie Mogul Backyard FX- http://www.youtube.com/show/backyardfx
Tom Antos- http://www.youtube.com/user/polcan99
Medieval Hollywood-
http://www.youtube.com/user/MedievalHollywood
Indie Action Tutorials-
http://www.youtube.com/user/ShahuyenProductions
Freddie Wong (look for his tutorials)-
http://www.youtube.com/show/freddiew
Epic Tutorials for iPhone -
http://www.youtube.com/user/EpicTutorialsDotCom
BAMMO- http://www.youtube.com/user/bammo?feature=watch
Film Skills- http://www.youtube.com/user/FilmSchoolOnDVD
Indiefone- http://www.youtube.com/user/indieFone
Youtube Filmmaking Channel-
http://www.youtube.com/channel/HCOHLWYjamGPU

Individual Videos

How to Shoot a Scene- http://www.youtube.com/watch?v=IK2IAEO-FUI

A Guide to Basic Cinematography- http://www.youtube.com/watch?v=gQnKGXHbgMA

Home-Made Boom Mic- http://www.youtube.com/watch?v=qmX3nbD8XJ4

Low-Budget Film Lighting- http://www.youtube.com/watch?v=gXRm9s_7ayQ

Simple Camera Trick (for tripods)- http://www.youtube.com/watch?v=Lz2q5y0HCC8

The Merricam No Cost DIY Steadycam- http://www.youtube.com/watch?v=JW6AWmqa8ZM

Filmic Pro Setting up the Shot- http://www.youtube.com/watch?v=JW6AWmqa8ZM

10 Household Hacks for Filmmakers- http://www.youtube.com/watch?v=-WX1DU74P6E

Simple Tips to Becoming a Better Editor- http://www.youtube.com/watch?v=XafunNmwtPg

Filmmaking 101- www.youtube.com/watch?v=Nz5zQt5QO3Y

Audio Resources

When it comes to hunting for audio resources on the Internet, you need to understand two terms- Royalty Free, and Creative Commons.

Royalty Free means essentially the music or effects are free for anyone to use in anything (including things that will make money) without you having to pay the creators anything. They're offered for you to do what you want with, although it's generally good practice to at least give them credit in your project credits list.

Creative Commons is an alternate Internet copyright system where people license their creative works for other people to use freely, but with some limitations. Each thing licensed under Creative Commons rules has a few simple requirements that you have to follow to use that thing in your project. The most common license is *Attribution-NonCommercial-Sharealike* license, which basically means you have to give them credit, you can't use it in anything that makes money, and you have to make your work Creative Commons as well when you release it. If this doesn't work for you, then you'd better find something else to use. However, not all Creative Commons items use this license, some just want credit and don't care what you do with it, so read carefully, and when in doubt write to the creator and ask them if you can use their work.

Places to Get Free Sound Effects

Freesound.org- A giant collection of work by amateur sound designers and people who love playing with audio. Make sure you credit their sounds though, as they're often Creative Commons, not Royalty Free.

SoundJay.com- another free Sound Effects site, these sounds are Royalty Free.

Flashkit.com- meant for game developers, but free FX are free FX!

TheFreeSite.com- maintains a directory of free sound effects sites for you to access at http://www.thefreesite.com/Free_Sounds/Free_WAVs/

Stonewashed.net- has a directory of free sound FX sites at http://stonewashed.net/sfx.html

Epicsound.com- Is is site where people trade ideas for how to make your own Sound Effects. If you're feeling DIY, then check it out!

Places to Get Free Music

Incompetech.com - Kevin Mcleod is an aspiring composer who puts all his stuff out there Royalty Free. A great place to get music, but be sure to credit him!

Youtube Audio Library- Youtube has recently created a library for amateur video producers to use in their videos so they don't get pulled down for copyright reasons. There are a few hundred songs there now, and it's growing! http://www.youtube.com/audiolibrary

Newgrounds.com Audio Portal- a huge collection of free music by aspiring musicians that you can use in your projects if you give them credit. Be careful to read the rules for using each song, and that the song isn't just their remake of a professional song. Some really talented composers on here, though. http://www.newgrounds.com/audio/

CreativeCommons.org- The Creative Commons site itself maintains a directory of other sites where you can find free music for your projects. Check out their list of sites at http://creativecommons.org/music-communities

www.ingramcontent.com/pod-product-compliance
Lightning Source LLC
Chambersburg PA
CBHW020529160726
47992CB00005BA/2318